Transformation

"Behold, I make all things new" (Rev. 21:5).

Also by Jim Ayer
Second Chance
Your Daily Journey to Transformation

Sandy,
Thank you for
lending me your books
to read—They were very
good reading. Sorry to be so
slow in returning Them. Thank you
again. love
xo
Shirley

Transformation

"Behold, I make all things new" (Rev. 21:5).

Jim Ayer

REVIEW AND HERALD® PUBLISHING ASSOCIATION
Since 1861 | www.reviewandherald.com

Review and Herald® titles may be purchased in bulk for educational, business, fund-raising, or sales promotional use. For information, e-mail specialmarkets@reviewandherald.com.

The Review and Herald® Publishing Association publishes biblically based materials for spiritual, physical, and mental growth and Christian discipleship.

Unless otherwise noted, Scripture references are taken from the New King James Version. Copyright © 1979, 1980, 1982 by Thomas Nelson, Inc. Used by permission.

Scripture quotations credited to GW are taken from *God's Word*. Copyright 1995 God's Word to the Nations. Used by permission of Baker Publishing Group. All rights reserved.

Bible texts credited to TEV are from the *Good News Bible*—Old Testament: Copyright © American Bible Society 1976; New Testament: Copyright © American Bible Society 1966, 1971, 1976.

Statement in this volume attributed to other speakers/writers are included for the value of the individual statements only. No endorsment of those speakers'/writers' other works or statements is intended or implied.

This book was
Edited by Anthony Lester
Copyedited by Delma Miller
Cover designed by David Berthiaume
Interior Design by Review and Herald® Design Center
Typeset: Minion Pro 11/13

PRINTED IN U.S.A.

17 16 15 14 13   5 4 3 2 1

Library of Congress Cataloging-in-Publication Data
Ayer, Jim, 1948-   .
   Transformation : "behold, I make all things new." / Jim Ayer.
      pages cm
1. Christian life. I. Title.
   BV4501.3.A95 2013
   248.4'86732—dc23
                              2012049326

ISBN 978-0-8280-2711-3

Dedication

To Janene,
my wonderful wife

Our many years together have been a growing friendship, anchored in a love that continues to blossom in Christ. And because of your dedication to our eternal partnership, I have been enabled, sustained, and encouraged to travel across this world spreading our Lord's amazing message of hope and love and revealing His plan to transform us into His image.

Contents

A Note From the Author

Steve Jobs, the former president of Apple, Inc., had an amazing ability to focus on his vision and make it become a reality. Few people would deny that he revolutionized the world, changing your life and mine in myriad ways. In the process Jobs became exceedingly rich. He was a man who had everything—everything, that is, except the one thing of greatest importance.

It was once said of him, "Steve Jobs transformed human existence with his technology, but he never figured out why humans exist. He never figured out whether there is a God. . . . Even Steve Jobs himself knew there was a missing component to his extraordinarily successful life."*

You might not have had a chance to change the world yet, but that doesn't mean you shouldn't be asking yourself whether or not there is a missing component in your life. In fact, you might even be a Christian who still feels there should be much more to your experience. Well, if your understanding of and involvement with God are like that of most other Christians, you probably are missing something.

In fact, not that long ago I was a Christian who was missing something in my life.

A former Buddhist monk in Nepal once shared with me, "Although I was a monk for much of my life, I had no inner peace. Then one day, while listening to the radio, I heard about Jesus. My life changed forever! As a Christian I now have peace."

But as a professed Christian, I didn't have this peace. Oh, I would put on a happy face for the watching world, for the church, and for my family, but at night I would crash beside my bed in tears. A sulking heap of despair, I would cry out, "Lord, I am so sorry. I have sinned against You *again!* I know I promised You yesterday that it would be different today, but . . . Lord, help me! I feel so guilty. I want to stop!"

This ugly ritual was repeated on an almost daily basis. I could never seem to get past my sins, as if they had powerful tentacles wrapped tightly around me, squeezing the very life out of me. My prayers for help seemed to reach no higher than the ceiling. I found it difficult to experience lasting victory and peace in Christ.

Do you feel this same way? Is something missing in your experience with God—robbing you of the joy and hope that the Bible says can be yours?

If you do feel this burden on your heart, I have great news. Even in this dark world that shuns God more often than not, I want to share with you the hope and the power that are available to transform you. Yes, victory and happiness are within your grasp today! Now is the time for the darkness of guilt and the crushing weight of sin to be cast from you by the awe-inspiring power of God.

It's time for you to walk with your head held high as a child of the King, working and living in His love, grace, and victory-enabling power. Christ's promise to His people is a promise to you: "To those who win the victory I will give the right to sit beside me on my throne, just as I have been victorious and now sit by my Father on his throne" (Rev. 3:21, TEV).

Imagine it! To those who overcome the temptations of this world as Christ overcame them—through God's almighty power—He has already granted the privilege of a place on His throne.

What do you say? It's time to start your royal training, isn't it? That's what this book is all about: leading you to a transformed life.

As you read, contemplate, and apply the liberating ideas and tools herein, it is my prayer that you will discover what the devil doesn't want you to discover: daily victory in Christ. True peace will soon flood your life, and you will be walking freer and happier than you ever imagined possible this side of heaven.

Jim Ayer

---

* *The Philadelphia Trumpet,* January 2012.

Introduction:

Stockholm Syndrome

Her name was plastered across the nightly news for weeks on end. Jaycee Lee Dugard, a girl who had been kidnapped and held as a sex slave, was now found after nearly 20 years. It was a sordid, sad, and tragic tale, but as events unfolded and reports became clear, a strange story began to emerge . . .

"Time and again during the 18 harrowing years she allegedly spent in captivity, Jaycee Lee Dugard must have had the chance to cry for help. She assisted her alleged abductor, Phillip Garrido, with his home business, sorting out orders by phone or e-mail. She occasionally greeted customers alone at the door. She even went out in public. But she apparently never made a run for it, returning each day instead to a shed in the backyard of the man who allegedly kidnapped and raped her. 'Jaycee has strong feelings with this guy,' her stepfather Carl Probyn—who saw Dugard snatched at age 11 from a bus stop in 1991—said Aug. 28. 'She really feels it's almost like a marriage.' "*

What happened to little Jaycee? How was it that she couldn't bring herself to escape the cruel, evil man who held her for nearly two decades? One answer, perhaps of many answers, could be a phenomenon known as Stockholm syndrome.

Nils Bejerot was the man who coined the term. A criminologist and psychiatrist living in Sweden, he was called upon to serve as an adviser to the police on a bizarre case. In 1973 employees of a local bank in Stockholm, Sweden, were held at gunpoint by robbers for six days. When their harrowing ordeal finally came to an end, however, the hostages were apparently so emotionally attached to their captors that they refused to testify against the criminals in court.

Another intriguing case involved newspaper heir Patty Hearst. While attending college in Berkeley, California, in February 1974, she was kidnapped by the terrorist gang known as the Symbionese Liberation Army (SLA).

Held captive in a closet and reportedly raped regularly, she strangely transformed into a willing member of the SLA. A famous photo of Patty, who changed her name to Tania while with the group, was taken during the Hibernia Bank holdup in San Francisco. It shows a gun-wielding Tania seemingly supporting her new allegiance to the radical terror group.

After killing many of the SLA's members, the police eventually caught up to Hearst in a San Francisco safe house. Her criminal trial began on February 4, 1976, and ended with a verdict of guilty and a seven-year prison sentence. After 22 months President Jimmy Carter commuted her sentence, and in 2001 President Bill Clinton gave her a full pardon—ending the astonishing ordeal of a kidnap victim.

The lives of Patty Hearst, Jaycee Lee Dugard, and a half-dozen bank hostages were completely altered by the wicked acts of devious minds preying upon them. And as hard as it might be to believe, at some point during their individual ordeals, these captives actually began to experience positive feelings toward those who harmed them.

Now, here's a thought to ponder: This is not unlike what has happened to you, me, and the rest of the human race. We were abducted long ago and have since been held captive by the devil and his minions on this dark planet for thousands of years. And far worse than that: after having been deceived into rejecting our true home in Paradise, we've been under the iron fist of Satan and his cohorts for so long that we have developed an affinity for them and their plans for this world. Like Jaycee, we've found reasons not to run from our captors; like Patty Hearst, we've become willing participants in sin.

Yet even now, we aren't without hope. We've been given an opportunity to escape! But wait—our opportunity goes way beyond that. Even though Patty Hearst was guilty of bank robbery and other nefarious activities, she received a full pardon from the leader of the nation. In the same way, as a Christian, you've been given a full pardon from the leader of the universe.

However, it is absolutely crucial that you take hold of this opportunity to escape these captors, who continue to do you great harm and who will eventually destroy you if you don't act. Satan is doing everything he can to make you a brainwashed victim of Stockholm syndrome, to get you to miss seeing the true path to freedom.

It's sad, really, yet true—it's quite possible that the devil's brainwashing has taken place over such an extended period of time that you might be totally unaware of what has actually happened to you and the nature of your true identity.

Let me start fixing that right now: You are royalty, as a matter of fact, and heir to the riches of the universe. Even better, God has a plan to free you and redeem you to your rightful place in His realm.

A man named Max discovered this plan, and he is rejoicing today. We'll take a look at his story next.

---

* Laura Fitzpatrick, "Stockholm Syndrome," *Time,* Aug. 31, 2009.

Chapter 1

Mad Max

A man of few words, Max was the kind of guy who would just as soon kill you as look at you. If you spotted him on the road heading in your direction, you would go out of your way to avoid him if you wanted to live.

The police in Papua New Guinea had been on Max's trail for a long time, but they were finally able to close in on him, apprehending him without a fight. They tossed him in prison and thought that was the end of their troubles.

Not so fast, boys; stopping Max wasn't going to be that easy.

During his first week in prison, Max noticed that the prisoners who attended church services on Sunday didn't have to work on that day. *H'mmm. If I attend church, I won't have to work on Sunday either.* It didn't take long for him to decide to go to church on Sunday. Then the following week, he became aware of another group—a congregation of Seventh-day Adventists—that attended church on Saturday and, well, guess what? They didn't have to work on Saturday.

Max was soon attending church every Saturday and Sunday.

However, he received little other benefit from the services. His character was left unscathed, as within three weeks of attending his first service, he and two other inmates broke out of prison. Not long after, they were on their way to the most notorious area of Papua New Guinea, a mountainous region that had earned its reputation because it was infested with every type of criminal one could imagine.

When Max and his partners in crime made it to the top of one mountain, he said to them, "Let's build a Christian church. If the police think we got religion, maybe they will leave us alone." The question was What denomination would their new church be? Max began to reason with the others, "If we say we are Lutherans, no one will believe us, because everyone in the region is a Lutheran. But if we say we are Seventh-day Adventists, they will believe us, because everyone here hates the Adventists." They were soon all in agreement, so construction on the new church began.

A few weeks passed, and a new Seventh-day Adventist church sign hung above the door of their rustic wooden church. Max also constructed a trapdoor in the center of the church floor; it led to a secret tunnel that wound down the mountain to the ravine below. This offered him the perfect getaway opportunity should the police arrive looking for the three fugitives. It also provided the ideal location to store their weapons, including Max's AK-47.

The work was finally done, just in time for church on Saturday! As the three-man congregation sat on the tree-trunk pews, they realized that someone was needed to conduct the services. "Simple," Max said to the others. "There are three of us, so one will do the youth service, another will do Sabbath school, and I'll do the church service." His buddies agreed that it was a good plan, but there was still a problem . . .

They left the church and, a short time later, reappeared wearing new ties and carrying three Bibles. You see, it just didn't feel right to them to have church and not wear a tie and have a Bible—so they had gone out and stolen them before the service started.

For several weeks the men continued their little charade until, one day, word drifted down to the large Lutheran school in the valley. It was the only Christian school in the area, so many Adventist parents sent their youth to attend the school out of necessity—even though the leadership was somewhat antagonistic toward them. The young Adventists said, "Let's attend church there this week." They all agreed and started up the mountain on Saturday.

As the fugitives were sitting in church, looking quite dashing in their stolen ties and holding their stolen Bibles, a knock came at the church door. *Could it be the police? Should we grab our guns?* Then they heard laughter. *Who could it be?* Max opened the door and was greeted by a multitude of smiling young faces. "Who are you?" he growled.

"We are Adventists from the valley. We came to worship with you today."

Max was in a pinch. He invited the group in, but he had no idea how to conduct a service; his only exposure to church had been for three weeks in jail. Even then, he hadn't paid any attention. "You're the guests," he improvised. "Why don't you conduct services?"

"Sure! We'd be happy to," responded the vibrant youth. In the following weeks, this was the pattern, an arrangement the men actually began to enjoy.

Then one Saturday morning the men waited and waited, but no young people showed up to church. *Where are our new friends?* It wasn't very long before the criminal network was in high gear, and word arrived from the valley. "Max," said the messenger, "the principal of the Lutheran school chained the gate, locking in the Adventists. They cannot attend your services."

Upon hearing this, Max flew into a violent rage. He threw back the pews, reached down to the floor, and flung open the trapdoor. He clamored down the stairs, grabbed his AK-47, and headed out. His anger uncontrolled, his finger tightened around the cold trigger. As he stormed down the mountainside, a loud report wailed from the barrel of his gun as he blasted a clump of bananas in the trees.

Reaching the gate of the school, he was confronted with a huge chain held firmly together by a padlock. A rapid 10 rounds from his assault rifle made short work of the lock. Max was through the gate.

"Where are you?" His words echoed through the emptied halls of the school. The gun-wielding madman stormed from classroom to classroom looking for the principal, who was cowering under a desk in an office.

It wasn't long before Max discovered his prey.

Now jamming the barrel of his gun against the chest of the principal, Max shouted, "Where's my congregation?" They were certainly interesting words from the mouth of a lifelong criminal. Before the lips of the quivering principal could squeak out a response, Max continued, "You better release them, or I'll take it that we have a point of doctrinal dispute! Do you believe in hell? I'm not sure I do, but I'm going to send you there if you don't release my congregation—and I will meet you there shortly!"

Unsurprisingly, the principal agreed, and soon all the students were once again attending the otherwise-peaceful mountain church with the three escaped convicts. It also wasn't very long till their little church had spawned five additional study groups that met each week in other areas of the lawless mountain region.

One day the students came to Max and said, "We need to hold an evangelistic series." Max responded, "Sure! But what's an evangelistic series?" After a brief explanation, all agreed to the cause, so one of the young people called the nearest Adventist church mission station to see if someone would come to help them with the meetings.

"That area is far too dangerous," responded the mission president. "It's full of every type of evil person."

"Sir," responded the young caller, "Max and his friends say they will keep guard over the meetings. They have assured us that no harm will come to those who come to our meetings." The nervous president eventually relented.

A surprising number of people turned out for the meetings, and soon the crowd was witness to joyful baptisms. On the final night Max and his two jailbreak buddies were baptized by the mission president.

When someone later asked Max why he waited till the final night to be baptized, his reply was amusing: "Since I was in charge of security, I thought it would be wrong if I had to shoot someone if I was already baptized." That certainly is a curious reply, isn't it?

But Max is no longer the foul-tempered criminal he used to be. He has experienced an amazing change of lifestyle and character. In fact, largely because of his commitment to peaceful faith and Bible outreach, today this little "criminal church" has grown into two large churches with 10 weekly branch meetings in other locations.

What happened? What changed this hateful, evil person into a loving child of God? I don't believe science can explain it, but the Bible is literally bulging with information on a process that the apostle Paul calls transformation.

That's what happened to Max—he was transformed!

Before sharing the secrets of this fountain of God's transforming power, I'd like to give you a brief glimpse into another life that was drastically changed—mine. The ups and downs I experienced, my successes and my failures, led me to the amazing truths that I want to share with you in this book.

I had been brainwashed, a sufferer of Stockholm syndrome. Unlike Max's sudden transformation from criminal to Bible worker, the changes in my life came in fits of starts and stops. It all began one afternoon while I was high on drugs.

Chapter 2

True Encounter

Until that moment I had no idea who God was. But in the middle of my being high on marijuana, He interrupted me. "Jim, you have a short time to decide."

Who are you? What's going on? I had just experienced an encounter with the God of the universe, but it was hard for me to believe that He would stoop to talk to me.

The evidence had been right in front of me, however. I had just witnessed a conversation between God and the devil. It might seem strange for you to read, but it's true. Let me explain: I was transported, somehow, to a huge stadium where I was witness to a debate—a debate over me! The devil was listing every argument I had ever used to turn others on to drugs. He now presented to God those very arguments as his own. I was to be the prize.

The debate lasted only a short time, and in an instant I was back in my tiny room, stone-cold sober!

I didn't believe a simple drug reaction could have produced the surrealistic event that had just occurred. It was real, as was the voice that now spoke with powerful authority: "Jim, you have a short time to decide."

If I told you that you had a short time to decide, how long would you take to respond? A day or two, or maybe a week at most? I took two years! Yes, God gave me two years to work through the speed bumps in my life, but then it was time for me to make a decision.

"Jim! Tonight is your last night to decide."

The voice was even more powerful than the first time I had heard it. I had been partying all day long, and now God set before me the paths of life and death. The choices were very clear to me. I don't know how I knew it; I just did. I believe our home that night was full of heavenly angels and fallen angels doing battle over me.

I made the right choice.

I listened to the voices that were saying, "This is the way, walk in it" (Isa. 30:21). I grabbed all of my drugs and headed to the kitchen, where my wife, Janene, was changing our baby son. "Honey, I have to get rid of all this." She turned and smiled, not fully comprehending the gravity of the moment. Still grasping my deadly cargo, I headed for the bathroom.

I lifted the lid, dumped the drugs into the toilet, and pulled down on the chrome handle. *Swoosh.* In that instant I experienced the removal of a gigantic weight that had been crushing the spirit from my body. There came over me a sense of peace and relief that I cannot begin to describe. Tears flowed down my cheeks—tears of joy, relief, and happiness.

I don't know what you call this event. All I know is that I had carried a monster weight on my shoulders for most of my life, yet God said, "Here, Jim, give it to Me. I will deal with it for you." And when I did, indescribable joy came to me!

Hearing a noise behind me, I turned to see Janene standing in the doorway, quietly crying. I managed to choke out, "Would you join me in a prayer?"

She responded, "Yes." Arm in arm, we walked to the living room, where I pondered this astounding event for a moment.

I said softly, "God, I'm sorry it took so long." This sorrow over my stubborn delay inaugurated my journey of discovering what it really means to become a follower of Jesus. [1]

Unfortunately, I was a slow learner for a long time. God had to help me through many ups and downs over many long years. But the good news is that this long journey has prepared me to be able to share with you such great hope. If God was able to break through in my life, He can break through in your life.

And what a remarkable breakthrough! As God led me day by day, my study time in the Bible increased, as did the amount of time I spent in prayer. I simply could not get enough of Him. I was ravenous to know Jesus better, and as I studied and prayed, my ideas, habits, and personality began to change. The writer Ellen White makes an interesting note of this transformation process:

"Just as soon as there is the diligent study of the Bible that there should be, we shall not fail of noting a marked difference in the characters of the people of God. We shall say from the heart, 'The things I once loved, I now hate; and the things I once hated, I now love.' " [2]

The lies I once thought nothing of telling now stuck in my throat. The cuss words that so easily rolled from my tongue now halted long before they were uttered. The temper that once flared so easily now took longer to rise and, when it did, it stopped reaching the volcanic stage it once did.

The changes were slow but steady, sure—somewhat like climbing up several flights of stairs. I would arrive at a landing, catch my breath, and then proceed again. Indeed, for the most part, the Christian climb is nothing like attaching one's self to a rocket ship.

I once heard Billy Graham say, "I'd rather have one foot out of hell heading toward heaven than one foot out of heaven heading toward hell." It's really all about the direction you're heading. A steady upward ascent on the stairway to heaven is God's goal for us.

But before you think I was a perfect saint, I confess that once in a while I would slip and fall off of several flights of stairs, all at once, and it was never pretty.

---

[1] You can read more about our journey with God in the book *Second Chance*, copublished by Review and Herald Publishing Association and 3ABN Books.

[2] In *Review and Herald*, Apr. 9, 1889.

Chapter 3

Fall From Grace

Several years into my Christian experience I felt a strong call from the Lord to go into full-time ministry. This meant selling my business and home and moving to a college . . . somewhere. I never let a moment go by in which I didn't mention it to Janene. Until one day she said, "OK."

That was all I needed!

Soon after, I was handing over the keys to the business and home to a buyer, saying, "Send me the money when it closes escrow." Some might say that was a foolish move, but I was ready to drop everything to follow God's call!

But here's where it gets interesting. For several years I had been spending hours in prayer and study every single day; my life was a testimony to that fact. This former drug dealer, thief, liar, alcoholic, and more had been changed from the inside—enabled by God's mighty transformation power. I was so excited to be a Christian.

One evening while getting ready to conduct a prayer meeting at our church, I went next door to the home of a doctor who had been instrumental in getting me involved in his church. "Doctor," I said, "why don't you come to prayer meeting?" His response seemed both sad and strange to me at the time. "Jim, just wait till your kids are older and you need to work harder; you'll get tired, and then you will see why."

Well, I just couldn't imagine such a statement having any validity. *I'm so in love with Jesus*, I thought. *How could I ever miss prayer meeting?*

Talk about famous last words!

Not much longer after that conversation I became involved with various activities in the community, such as serving as the president of the local junior chamber of commerce. Unfortunately, there were plenty more opportunities in which to get involved. Each of these new ventures subtracted from my time with my Lord, in His Word and in prayer.

So by the time we loaded up the truck and headed to college to start my theology program, my spiritual growth had been on the skids for some time. That sounds strange, doesn't it? But it's true, and it happens to almost everyone at some point in their Christian walk. In fact, the devil will see to it that it happens.

Jesus actually addresses this potential fall from grace—potential because it doesn't have to happen—in Luke 15:8: "What woman, having ten silver coins, if she loses one coin, does not light a lamp, sweep the house, and search carefully until she finds it?"

This woman had saved 10 prized silver coins; she treasured each one of them. They were everything to her. I can almost see her taking them from their special box just to admire them, to hold each one, to recount them.

Yet one day, as she did her normal count, she came up short. In a state of stock, she shouted, "One is lost! Where is my coin?" She felt utter desperation. In those days, most homes in Israel had no windows and almost all had dirt floors—not very helpful conditions when searching for a small lost coin.

She was persistent, however, and after searching every crack, crevice, and dirty corner, she finally found her lost coin. Then with tender care, she placed it back in her special box in its very special place.

Now it was time for a party! She let all of her neighbors know what had happened and invited them to rejoice with her. Her precious coin had been lost but now was found!

Did you notice where the coin was lost? It wasn't in a foreign country or in a strange city. She didn't lose it outside. It was lost within the confines of her home. Likewise, we can find ourselves lost even while in the church. A name on the church books is not a free ticket to heaven. Yes, we might have been in the church for years—our entire lives even—yet lose our connection with the Life-giver. Sometimes, we won't even know it has happened.

Satan's timing is astonishingly good. Shortly before I completed my theology degree, things fell apart with the transfer of my business and home. After some costly time with attorneys, we were again in control of our holdings, and it became my total focus.

Shortly after, the Nevada-Utah Conference president called me to say, "Jim, I would like you to become the pastor of a new church in my conference." It was my dream job, the reason I had gone to college!

But I responded, "No."

The reason was simple enough. I had quit studying God's Word and had stopped praying long enough that I could no longer hear the voice of the Shepherd saying, "This is the way, walk in it." The fact of the matter was that I had decided to stay where I was, and that meant I would not be going with God. We can't do both at the same time.

Instead of becoming a minister, I became a high-powered real-estate broker, a radio talk show host, and a Washington, D.C., political player. I soon had it all. I had the money, the influence, and the friends in high places—except the one Friend I really needed.

Praise God, He did not give up on me. While I was sitting in church one weekend, the same voice that had called out to me years before spoke once again, very distinctly saying, "Jim, the Holy Spirit could be poured out all around you, yet you will *never* recognize Him nor receive Him!"

Wow! That was plain enough.

It reminded me of my experience many years earlier when the Lord had said, "Jim, tonight is your last night to decide." At that moment I didn't want to hear what God was saying. It meant that although I was sitting in church looking like a highly successful businessman, all dressed up in my nice suit and giving large offerings, I was a lost coin in God's house.

Be honest—are you in the same boat as I was then? Is your time with God in prayer and study exciting? Or is it boring—or perhaps even nonexistent? Can you say, with certainty, that you have a ticket to board the H.M.S. *Hope*, which is soon to dock on the shores of eternity?

On that day many will cry out to the rocks and mountains, "Fall on us and hide us from the face of Him who sits on the throne and from the wrath of the Lamb! For the great day of His wrath has come, and who is able to stand?" (Rev. 6:16, 17). Still, others will shout, "Behold, this is our God; we have waited for Him, and He will save us. This is the Lord; . . . we will be glad and rejoice in His salvation" (Isa. 25:9).

What will you say on that day? How can you be sure?

When that crystal-clear message rang in my ears, two roads rose up before me—the very same roads I had gazed down that life-changing night years before. One road was life; the other was death. The same two choices in my life—*again!*

Praise the Lord that He is a God of second chances! He handed me an opportunity, and I grabbed it—*again!* When I did, life then and now has been nothing short of remarkable.

Your life can be better as well, fuller and more peaceful than ever before. Maybe you're thinking, *I've already had my second chance, possibly even my third chance.* Let me assure you that God will give you another chance as long as you earnestly desire and claim it. "The Lord God [is] merciful and gracious, longsuffering, and abounding in goodness and truth, keeping mercy for thousands, forgiving iniquity and transgression and sin" (Ex. 34:6, 7).

I love the word "longsuffering." It conveys a depth of patience on the part of God toward us that I'm sure will be our study for eternity. We're often ready to give up on even good friends for just one or two offenses, but God will always be ready to be our friend. You can trust this promise of God.

And remember Jesus' parables of the lost sheep and the lost son. Their meanings should not be missed. Each parable represents people who have been part of the church family. The sheep had wandered away from the church and had no idea how to get back, and the son chose to walk away.*

So the great news is that our loving Lord doesn't give up on anyone. He searches the house for the coin, He scours the countryside for the sheep, and He patiently waits for the form of His son to reappear on the horizon.

In each case, we find Him in celebration—holding the coin with tender love, gently placing the sheep over His shoulders, and reaching out with nail-pierced hands to embrace the lost son in His forgiving arms.

God was so patient with me. He still is. And He will be with you as well. It is the devil who whispers in your ear there is no hope for you. The more depressed, discouraged, and despondent you become, the better he likes it. So don't listen to him. He is a liar. Forgiveness, grace, and power— the kind of help capable of transforming you—are available to you on a God-sized scale!

To illustrate this spiritual warfare, God drew back the spiritual veil, providing us with a spectacular view of the unseen dimension. Past the curtain, we see Joshua in service as God's high priest, but the devil is accusing him of being too filthy to serve God. "He showed me Joshua the high priest standing before the Angel of the Lord, and Satan standing at his right hand to oppose him. And the Lord said to Satan, 'The Lord rebuke you, Satan! The Lord who has chosen Jerusalem rebuke you! *Is* this not a brand plucked from the fire?'" (Zech. 3:1, 2).

Notice where Satan is standing: right beside Joshua. This should give us pause. Where does the devil work? At our shoulder. He and his evil angels are watching us, speaking to us, and fighting for our allegiance. But you also need to know that according to the Bible, God wins in the end! That's right; God is all-powerful.

What you should be concerned about is whose side you're on right now. Who are you choosing to walk shoulder to shoulder with on a daily basis? This is how God handles the accusations and threats against His servants:

"Joshua was clothed with filthy garments, and was standing before the Angel. Then He answered and spoke to those who stood before Him, saying, 'Take away the filthy garments from him.' And to him He said, 'See, I have removed your iniquity from you, and I will clothe you with rich robes' " (verses 3, 4).

God took away Joshua's filth, and He offers to take away the filth of anyone else who is willing. This includes Max the convict, Jim Ayer the lost church member, and you.

But . . . there are urgent biblical principles we must understand and apply in order to celebrate our final victory on the shores of eternity. You're reading this book because that's what you want in your life, so let's get started!

---

* Be sure to read Luke 15:3-32!

Chapter 4

Power Play

Transformation builds idea upon idea. Each chapter sets out to build upon the previous with the ultimate goal, by the end, to offer you a strong foundation in your relationship with Christ. I believe that when you integrate this material into your life, you will be able to stand against every assault of the devil, through the power of God's grace, no matter the strength of the storm that beats against you.

But we need to be patient and make sure we cover all our bases as we move forward.

Have you ever heard the expression "What is past is prologue"? It means that what happened in the past lays the foundation for what happens today. For instance, a child that is the victim of physical beatings by a drunk, angry father might one day himself become a violent abusive father. Well, that's what we find in human nature. As we plot a course that will fill the sin-burrowed hole in our hearts, we need to look back to the beginning to understand why humans do what we do—why we sin against God in spite of ourselves.

Ironically, as we begin at the beginning, I want to take you to the last book of the Bible—Revelation. You might be familiar with Revelation already, but I want to show it to you in a way you might not have considered in the past.

For instance, in Revelation 12:7, 8, we find words describing heaven that seem totally out of place for what we typically consider to be a peaceful paradise: "And war broke out in heaven: Michael and his angels fought with the dragon; and the dragon and his angels fought, but they did not prevail, nor was a place found for them in heaven any longer."

Strange indeed: a war in heaven!

We can trust the Bible, and we do well to believe it, yet a war in heaven raises obvious questions. What happened in that once peaceful and happy place? Why did Lucifer no longer fit in? Verse 9 provides an indication:

"So the great dragon was cast out, that serpent of old, called the Devil and Satan, who deceives the whole world; he was cast to the earth, and his angels were cast out with him."

Scholars differ on whether this war was outright combat or a war of conflicting ideas, but one thing is certain: The struggle for supremacy eventually spilled over to Planet Earth. "We do not wrestle against flesh and blood, but against principalities, against powers, against the rulers of the darkness of this age, against spiritual hosts of wickedness in the heavenly places" (Eph. 6:12).

For our discussion, we need not delve into the details of what brought about the antagonistic deportment on the part of the fallen angels. We can surmise, however, that if God had not given them the free will to do it, the struggle would have never happened in the first place. That might sound like an ideal compromise to many people—removing a being's free will to ensure peace and safety for others.

But it would also mean that heaven would have been populated with mindless automatons incapable of experiencing genuine love. It is impossible for love to be received by mindless drones; it is also impossible for drones to share genuine love.

This means that true love for God could emanate only from beings who had free will. And we know this is what God wants, because "God is love" (1 John 4:8). He wants our obedience not because it's the only possible thing we could do, as slaves might, but because we love Him too much not to obey Him.

When God created Adam and Eve, this was His plan. They would love Him for who He was and choose to follow Him out of that love.

God's plan of peace and Paradise enraged Satan, once known as Lucifer, the "son of the morning" (Isa. 14:12), the most powerful created being in the universe and the leader of the failed revolt in heaven. It's unbelievable to think that he had once been God's emissary, standing in His fiery and glorious presence, and still chose to rebel. But however it happened, he now focused his complete wrath, envy, and hatred on destroying God's plans for the human race by turning Adam and Eve against the Creator.

This was the setting into which that first couple appeared on the scene.

Despite the war caused by the abuse of free will, Adam and Eve were supplied a full measure of independence. God knew that their genuine happiness was possible only if He could receive their love based upon the exercise of that free choice. Love could not be extracted by force, so Adam and Eve would be given the freedom and the opportunity to reject God.

And when given his opportunity to plead his sinister case to Adam and Eve, Satan came for them with all guns blazing. However, God did not leave the couple defenseless or ignorant of the conflict. He must have spent hours briefing them on the war in heaven and how they could avoid that clear and present danger. They would have known that Satan had already dragged down a third of the angels with him, causing them to be cast out of heaven, and if he had anything to do with it, Adam and Eve would be next![1]

Their choice came down to one small test of loyalty to God, who explained, "If you love Me, stay away from the tree of the knowledge of good and evil." Many Bible scholars believe that this tree was the only location on the entire planet where Satan was allowed to interact with human beings.[2] Of course, all this has been a very simplified version of these events, but this is really what the controversy boiled down to.

Even with God's counsel freshly planted in Eve's ears, she apparently wandered away from Adam's side and found herself beside the tree, speaking with a beguiling serpent. It was there that the devil began to erode her foundation and trust in God's Word. He had inhabited the body of a glorious serpent and engaged his prey in delightful conversation. Mesmerized, Eve would soon believe that a snake was more concerned for her happiness than God was.

Satan then led her to be transfixed by that beautiful tree. *Look at the size and color of that fruit—how wonderful it must be!* Although she had been provided with an unimaginable selection of beautiful and delicious fruit in the garden, she began to fantasize what else could be hers. The tentacles of evil were gaining a hold on her. She was at the edge of a giant pit, the bank crumbling away.

Yet sadly she not only bought the lie and defied the command of God—she became a salesperson for the archdeceiver and sold the same sad lie to Adam.

After they chose to ignore God's warnings, it took very little time for them to discover the awful consequences of their actions. By then it was too late to turn back; they had failed the test and, by their own choices, had thrown away the glorious light of their righteousness and replaced it with the darkness of Satan's cruelty and evil.

By their choice the entire human race had been effectively kidnapped—stolen from our true Father to serve the father of evil. Adam and Eve were now lost, their access to eternity ripped away, and they knew the sentence that awaited them: "In the day that you eat of it you shall surely die" (Gen. 2:17).

A terrible chill must have run through the bones of the once-happy couple. They had actually assisted Satan in a staggering victory! A celebration sprang up in the camp of the fallen; demons howled with glee. Satan's stealthy power play had been on display for the universe to behold; the tide of opinion seemed to be ebbing his way.

But while the devil had won an important battle, it was only just the beginning of the bigger conflict to come.

Satan saw that Jesus was calling out to the couple.[3] *Had He come to kill them?* The arch-demon drew near to eavesdrop on that conversation. By now he would have seen that Jesus carried with Him two lambs, and what happened next took him by complete surprise. Jesus took hold of the innocent lambs and killed them. No one in the universe had ever witnessed death. It was a horrifying and strange act. Jesus then took the skins of the lifeless lambs and wrapped them around Adam and Eve. Jesus then set forth a plan of salvation not only to the terrified couple but also to the awestruck universe.

Someday in the future, Jesus would lay down His kingly robes and descend to earth as a helpless human infant. Where Adam and Eve failed, He would overcome. His life would be one of complete victory over sin. No temptation hurled at Him would be fruitful. He would then offer Himself as a spotless sacrificial lamb, to be hung on a cruel cross, to pay the full penalty of Adam's and Eve's sins and for the sins of every soul who would accept His gift.

The offer was on the table, but Adam and Eve still had to act upon it. Still, they had a huge problem. They had given away their choice to Satan. They could do nothing; Satan controlled them. What now?

Jesus then turned in the direction of the devil. He said, "Because you have done this, you are cursed more than all cattle, and more than every beast of the field; on your belly you shall go, and you shall eat dust all the days of your life" (Gen. 3:14). John Wesley, commenting on this scene in his explanatory notes, observes that this "is part of the serpent's curse. A perpetual reproach is fastened upon him. Under the cover of the serpent he [Satan] is here sentenced to be . . . degraded and accursed of God."

It is critical to understand that although Satan inflicts great pain and suffering during the war, winning many battles along the way, he is not going to win the war. God, the Creator of the serpent, is in control. Although we are living in enemy territory during this temporary time of trial and tragedy prior to the grand finale, make no mistake—God wins!

And more than that, God wants us to defect from the devil's legions and join Him in the war. But how could Adam and Eve join a war against their newly appointed slave master? Jesus would provide them with His own mighty indwelling power to resist the devil. He would not only die on their behalf, but would also become their internal power source, enabling them to overcome every wicked onslaught. Still focused on Satan, Jesus explained, "*I will put enmity between you [Satan] and the woman*, and between your seed and her Seed; He shall bruise your head, and you shall bruise His heel" (verse 15).

God offered Adam and Eve "enmity," the indwelling power of God, to resist the devil's temptations. He also pounded a nail into Satan's prophetic coffin. In the future the deceiver would receive a deathblow to the head, a signal that God would ultimately win the war begun in heaven.

Of course, today that war still rages across our planet. The fierce anger that was spawned in the heart of Lucifer is at full blaze now, because he knows he has only a short time before his destruction. Never forget, Satan is an intelligent theologian who knows the Bible and can discern the steady tread of events.

As this war is waged across the landscape of human history, God pursues those who, exercising their free will, resolve to surrender to Him and allow the enmity to fortify their hearts against evil.

This is indeed the epic story of God's power to forgive, cleanse, and, best of all, transform us into His image! The devil would like us to forget this power, a power that causes him and his evil band to tremble—a power that we must understand, appreciate, and allow to work within us.

Unfortunately, the devil has been very successful, even causing many in the church to believe his lies. Check out the results of a survey conducted by the Barna Group, published January 9, 2012, under the title "What People Experience in Churches":

"The survey also probed the degree to which people say their lives had been changed by attending church. Overall, one quarter of Americans (26 percent) who had been to a church before said that their life had been changed or affected 'greatly' by attending church. Another one fourth (25 percent) described it as 'somewhat' influential. Nearly half said their life had not changed at all as a result of churchgoing (46 percent)."

It's hard to imagine, but almost half of churchgoers say they've experienced no change in their lives resulting from attending church. The lies of the devil are powerful!

Yet God has big plans for you. Satan chose to throw away his heavenly home, but you can still choose to align yourself with God's love and indwelling power to become an overcomer. Jesus says, "Behold, I stand at the door and knock. If anyone hears My voice and opens the door, I will come in to him and dine with him, and he with Me. To him who overcomes I will grant to sit with Me on My throne, as I also overcame and sat down with My Father on His throne" (Rev. 3:20, 21).

At this very moment, God is calling you from danger to safety. But you might be wondering, "How does He call me? How can I even hear Him?"

---

[1] Revelation 12:4 says, "His tail drew a third of the stars of heaven and threw them to the earth."

[2] Genesis 2:17 explains, "Of the tree of the knowledge of good and evil you shall not eat, for in the day that you eat of it you shall surely die."

[3] Some Bible scholars assert that Jesus, in His prehuman form, was the one who walked and interacted with the couple after the Fall, as they would be unable to live in God's presence.

Chapter 5

From Danger to Safety, Part 1

As the war that had begun in heaven raged on, the devil appeared to be winning. Adam and Eve watched in sorrow as the passing centuries multiplied evil's hold upon the human race, beginning with the murder of their beloved son Abel.

Death also began to whisper in the ears of the couple, telling them it was almost time for their sleep. The grave would indeed offer them a welcome respite from the agonizing years since their fall. If only they had listened to God cautioning them of the danger of sin, if only they had heeded those warnings, they would have been safe!

As you read through Scripture, you will often come upon this pattern of warning in the Bible. In each case God calls a prophet to warn earth's inhabitants that the effects of their sin have become too destructive. In this chapter I want to look at some examples of how God has delivered these warnings through His prophets. You'll see an awesome pattern emerge! First, He delivers a major prophecy as a warning to His people. Then, when the celestial alarm clock sounds on that prophecy, He raises up another prophet who confirms that prophecy and appeals to a new generation of God's people to heed that warning message.

While it is not my intent to provide an in-depth study on these prophecies, but rather to focus on how God uses prophets to guide His children and gather them away from danger, it is my intent to show you in short order that this pattern you're about to see has been repeated for our time. Yes! God is right now calling us out from the bondage of sin. You're going to be amazed, so let's get started.

Enoch and Noah

Enoch was born a full seven generations after the arrival of Adam and Eve in the Garden of Eden. However, because of the vitality and long life spans of the human race at the time, he might have had the opportunity to hear the sorrowful tale of the Fall from the lips of Adam himself. He might have even been witness to the angels brandishing swords of flame, barring all who would attempt to enter the Paradise of God, the former home of the human race.

Sadly, as earth's population rapidly increased, so did the evil desires of their hearts. Genesis 6:5 explains that "the Lord saw that the wickedness of man was great in the earth, and that every intent of the thoughts of his heart was only evil continually." This is the power of sin in the great arc of human history and the arc of a single human life. It grows and grows until it totally consumes. If only Adam and Eve had listened!

There were, however, men and women such as Enoch who chose the "enmity" promised by Jesus in the garden. This enmity fortified God's people against the flood of evil. In fact, the Bible records that "Enoch walked with God" (Gen. 5:22).

Many Bible commentators assert that Enoch was heaven's prophet in that day, shining brightly amid the moral darkness that consumed humanity. He delivered the Lord's message of hope and obedience to the masses. It was surely strong undiluted medicine, but it was calculated to call them from danger to safety.

Enoch warned as many people as he possibly could with these words: "Behold, the Lord comes with ten thousands of His saints, to execute judgment on all, to convict all who are ungodly among them of all their ungodly deeds which they have committed in an ungodly way, and of all the harsh things which ungodly sinners have spoken against Him" (Jude 14, 15).

Around the time Enoch turned 65 years old, God gave him a dramatic prophecy that would be a harbinger of a soon-coming nightmare for anyone who refused Enoch's testimony. The prophecy to the sin-laden world was delivered through the name of a child: Methuselah, the son of Enoch.

Methuselah means "When I die, the coming." At first the full weight of the message was unclear—the coming of what?—yet sinful people would soon discover the answer. Still, in His mercy, the Lord would first offer the people evidence that He had the power to rescue those who would choose to follow Him.

Enoch walked with God for 365 years, and then one day, likely while experiencing a spiritual feast in the presence of his Lord, something wonderful happened. I imagine the Lord said something like this to His prophet: "Enoch, we have a wonderful friendship. You're closer to My home than you are to yours; why don't you just come home with Me?" The Bible says, "And Enoch walked with God; and he was not, for God took him" (Gen. 5:24). Enoch was translated straight to heaven!

Many years later God raised up another prophet, a man named Noah, to confirm the prophecy of Enoch and divulge the full meaning of "when I die, the coming." You see, when Methuselah died, a worldwide flood of waters would come to destroy earth's inhabitants.

Humanity had, since the time of Enoch, filled its cup of iniquity, and the stench rose all the way to heaven: "The earth also was corrupt before God, and the earth was filled with violence" (Gen. 6:11). God would bring a flood of water to extinguish sin and sinners before they had the opportunity to corrupt every living being and destroy Eden's redemption plan.

In your mind's eye, watch Noah standing side by side with Methuselah on the massive ramp leading into the ark. Large crowds had gathered to taunt the aging prophet. "Old man, you're crazy! It has never even rained!"

Then Noah answered, "This man standing next to me is 969 years old, the oldest man to have ever lived. But when he dies, God is going to destroy the earth and everyone who does not choose to enter the ark. Trust in these words; God's prophecies will never fail!"

Yet the taunts and jeers continued: "All things have gone on as they have since the beginning of time. Who are you to tell us any different?" While the venom still dripped from their lips, animals of every kind appeared on the horizon, moving toward the recently completed ark as if guided by an unseen hand.

Perhaps Methuselah collapsed on the wooden planks at that very moment. Noah quickly reminded his listeners a last time, "When he dies, the coming! Please come into the ark!" If they would heed his warning, they would be delivered from danger.

After Noah and his family entered the ark, an unseen hand closed the massive door behind them. Days passed as the taunts outside grew in intensity, but on the seventh day—rain. As the first drops fell, the mouths of the throng were stopped. No one could explain the phenomenon, but God's prophet had had the answer and they had refused to listen to him.

The heavens then shattered into pieces as cascades of water rushed to meet mighty torrents exploding up from the earth. Amid screams to open the door, the remnants of humankind attempted to cling to the floating ark, but to no avail. The planet was ripped apart; nature was turned out of its course. All was destroyed, save the ark and those inside who had heeded the prophet's warnings and followed him to safety.

Abram and Moses

As time passed, and the children of Noah repopulated the earth, the struggle between good and evil was far from over. Many of his descendants had turned away from God and turned toward strange gods, having forgotten how the Lord had saved their ancestors.

In the midst of this struggle, a man called Abram was living comfortably in Ur of the Chaldees when he was called upon by God. "Get out of your country, from your family and from your father's house, to a land that I will show you. I will make you a great nation; I will bless you and make your name great; and you shall be a blessing" (Gen. 12:1, 2).

By this time the average life span of a human being had dropped drastically from the pre-Flood age, so at 75 years old, Abram could have qualified as a card-carrying member of the AARP. Can you imagine, at that age, moving from the place and friends you love and traveling by camel to an unknown location? This is what God asked him to do, and it's exactly what Abram did.

As responsive as Abram was to God, we know he still had to go through an extended time of testing and growth before God's promise of making him a great nation could come true. But finally, the day arrived when 90-year-old Sarah gave birth to the child appointed by God to become the seed of the nation destined to become God's conduit of blessings to the world.

Yet, even as God had kept the covenant He had made with Abram, the Lord now revealed additional details regarding the nation He was to birth through Isaac: "Know certainly that your descendants will be strangers in a land that is not theirs, and will serve them, and they will afflict them four hundred years. And also the nation whom they serve I will judge; afterward they shall come out with great possessions" (Gen. 15:13, 14).

God delivered this prophecy to Abraham who, I'm sure, shared the information with his son and grandchildren. Its meaning was, perhaps, sketchy to him, but long after he died, at the appointed time, the fire of God's presence descended upon a bush in an uninviting wilderness desert, where He attracted the attention of a shepherd.

As the weatherworn keeper of sheep approached the bush, God spoke: "Do not draw near this place. Take your sandals off your feet, for the place where you stand is holy ground. . . . I am the God of your father—the God of Abraham, the God of Isaac, and the God of Jacob" (Ex. 3:5, 6). If the fire-laden yet unconsumed bush didn't get his attention, the voice of the Almighty did. Moses' sandals were off in an instant. I believe it is because he immediately recognized it to be the voice of God. For 40 years after fleeing Egypt to save his own life, Moses had the opportunity in his wilderness wanderings to listen to and recognize God's voice. In humble prayer and communion he had learned to know and follow that voice. God could now use Moses as His prophet.

The Lord said, "I have surely seen the oppression of My people who are in Egypt, and have heard their cry because of their taskmasters, for I know their sorrows. So I have come down to deliver them out of the hand of the Egyptians" (verses 7, 8). He offered Moses a part in that work. The 80-year-old had to decide whether he would stay where he was or go with God. This same decision comes to you and me, and we can't stay where we are and go with God.

After a little bit of resistance, Moses finally relented. He would confirm the prophecy God had delivered to Abram 430 years earlier; as God's prophet Moses would play an active role in its fulfillment.

The shepherd of the Jews soon made the arduous journey back to his birthplace, the mighty nation of Egypt. Once again he ascended the steps leading to courts of royalty, courts he was once in line to inherit. After numerous dramatic and mighty encounters with the stubborn pharaoh, Moses led the children of Israel out of bondage, forward to freedom, loaded down with the wealth of Egypt, just as God had prophesied: "It came to pass at the end of the four hundred and thirty years—on that very same day—it came to pass that all the armies of the Lord went out from the land of Egypt" (Ex. 12:41).

It's amazing! Forty years earlier Moses had thought himself a deliverer. The results were awful: He murdered an Egyptian, fled the nation to save his own life, and did not deliver a single slave. It's so much better when we join God in His work—isn't it?

But all was not a bed of roses for Moses and the children of Israel. Much of their time was occupied with complaining . . .

"Moses, we need water!"

"Moses, we're hungry!"

"Moses, if we only had the leeks and garlics of Egypt."

They didn't want to move. Then they wanted to move. Then they—

well, you get the idea. This rebellious spirit sprung up in the desert and then continued for generation after generation, until God delivered an ultimatum through the prophet Daniel.

Daniel and John the Baptist

Daniel had proved himself to be God's man again and again, and now the Lord entrusted him with a prophetic message that was to stretch 490 years into the future. This prophecy is actually the first portion (483 years) of a two-part prophecy:

"Seventy weeks are determined for your people and for your holy city, to finish the transgression, to make an end of sins, to make reconciliation for iniquity, to bring in everlasting righteousness, to seal up vision and prophecy, and to *anoint the Most Holy*. Know therefore and understand, that from the going forth of the command to restore and build Jerusalem *until Messiah the Prince*, there shall be seven weeks and sixty-two weeks. . . . And after the sixty-two weeks *Messiah shall be cut off*, but not for Himself."[1]

In this first part of a greater prophecy, which we'll look at a little later, God informs His chosen people that His patience regarding their long and sordid history of grievous sins was almost at an end. Unless they sought His righteousness with all their hearts, unless they permitted God to transform them, they would cease being His people. It was a clear message that even God's grace has its limits!

In His eternal love, God would give them one final opportunity as a nation to return to Him, delivering that message through Daniel's major time prophecy. He would send His Son, Messiah the Prince, to plead with them *in person*. He even pinpointed the date of His Son's arrival so no one would miss the event. The Messiah would then be anointed. (Jesus fulfilled this with His baptism.) Then the Messiah would be "cut off"—a reference to when Christ would be crucified on the cross.

The prophecy was given; the countdown clock was ticking. Historians know that the command to restore Jerusalem came in 457 B.C. This was the starting date from which the 69 weeks would be tabulated. Again, on the appointed day, 483 years later, the Messiah was to be anointed. Following His established pattern that we have already seen in this chapter, near the end of 483 years, God called forth a new prophet to confirm the prophecy. "Behold, I send My messenger before Your face, who will prepare Your way before You" (Mark 1:2).

For months a prophet clad in camel hair stood in stark contrast to the richly appareled church leaders who gathered around him. John the Baptist directed all of Israel to God's ultimatum: turn from sin and seek righteousness.

"John came baptizing in the wilderness and preaching a baptism of repentance for the remission of sins. Then all the land of Judea, and those from Jerusalem, went out to him and were all baptized by him in the Jordan River, confessing their sins" (verses 4, 5). A muddy, watery soup swirled at the feet of the young prophet as he made his way up the bank of the Jordon River. His powerful voice never missing a beat, hearts were touched, and many individuals indeed heeded the stinging reproofs and warnings of God's prophet. But as a nation, they were still rapidly falling further from God's amazing grace.

Most had come out of simple curiosity to catch a glimpse of John; others had come to put a halt to the troublous madman stirring up the people. As they listened, John suddenly stopped in mid-sentence and stared intently into the crowd; then he proclaimed, "I baptize with water, but there stands One among you whom you do not know" (John 1:26).

What a scene; what a moment! The One for whom all history had been waiting was standing among them. The eyes of John and Jesus finally connected in celestial embrace—time stood still for the man of God as he met his Creator face to face.[2] But the crowd, including the high church officials, did not know Him.

The celestial alarm clock had sounded—the Messiah was anointed (baptized), announcing His ministry to the world. The next alarm would sound in three and a half years, when the Messiah was "cut off" (crucified).

But even after they crucified Jesus, there would still be time for the Jewish nation to repent. According to the prophecy in Daniel 9:27, God allotted the Jewish people three and a half more years to know the Messiah and accept Him.

This clarion call was delivered to them by the disciples and the fledgling Christian church. Yet Israel's time as a nation was nearing its end. God spoke through Stephen the martyr, offering one final chance for the Jews to move from danger to safety. The response of the Jewish leadership? They stoned Stephen. At that moment the gospel was to be taken to the Gentiles.

The Next Prophet

I shared earlier that the 490 years of Daniel's prophecy was only the first part of a longer prophecy, but what is this larger prophecy? It's found in Daniel 8:14: "For two thousand three hundred days; then the sanctuary shall be cleansed."

To understand this prophecy, we need to go back to the period of time just after the Jews were freed from Egypt. While the nation of Israel sojourned in the desert, God provided Moses a set of construction plans for a portable building that was to house the Lord Himself.

God's directions were specific: "Let them make Me a sanctuary, that I may dwell among them. According to all that I show you, that is, the pattern of the tabernacle and the pattern of all its furnishings, just so you shall make it" (Ex. 25:8, 9). Isn't it wonderful to know that God's love is so vast that He desires to dwell with His people!

Yet not only would this structure be God's tabernacle among His people—it was also to be a living illustration of the work and mission of Jesus Christ, our high priest, and of earth's coming judgment.[3] "This is the main point of the things we are saying: We have such a High Priest, who is seated at the right hand of the throne of the Majesty in the heavens, a Minister of the sanctuary and of the true tabernacle which the Lord erected, and not man" (Heb. 8:1, 2).

According to Daniel 8:14, it is this sanctuary that was to be cleansed unto 2300 days. As I've already mentioned, we know that this prophetic time period is not literal days; only the day-for-a-year reckoning of Numbers 14:34 and Ezekiel 4:6 works to pinpoint, with precise accuracy, the beginning of Christ's public ministry, the date of His crucifixion, and the end of Israel as God's corporate people.

It only stands to reason, then, that the same reckoning of days to years should also apply to the greater prophetic time period of 2300 days of Daniel 8:14. But in case you're still in doubt, there is also another intriguing way to be sure that this period must be reckoned as years and not days. The following instruction was given to the people who encircled the tabernacle of God in the desert:

"The tenth day of this seventh month *shall be the Day of Atonement*. It shall be a holy convocation for you; *you shall afflict your souls*, and offer an offering made by fire to the Lord. And you shall do no work on that same day, for it is the Day of Atonement, to make atonement for you before the Lord your God. For any person who is not afflicted in soul on that same day shall be cut off from his people" (Lev. 23:27-29).

Let's first focus on the phrase "the Day of Atonement." If you were to ask a Jew about "the day," they would typically respond, "Why, it's the Day of Atonement." To the Jew, there is only one "the day." Hence, when Daniel wrote of 2300 days to his Jewish audience, it would naturally be understood as "2300 Days of Atonement"—or 2300 years, since "the day" was an event that happened once a year. It would take 2300 Days of Atonement, or 2300 years' worth of Days of Atonement, to fulfill this prophetic time period.

What is the Day of Atonement? Once each year, the Jewish high priest went into the Most Holy Apartment of the sanctuary and ministered on behalf of the Jewish people in the very presence of God. The deposited sins of the people were removed and cast upon the "scape goat," which was led from the camp to die alone in the wilderness.

On this day, it was critical for everyone in the camp to follow God's instruction to "afflict your souls." It was a day of judgment for the nation and for each individual, who needed to examine his or her life to ensure all of their sins had been forsaken and deposited on the sanctuary altar. If these sins were not left there for the high priest to transfer to the "scape goat," then a person was considered unclean, polluted by sin, and must leave the camp. Sin could not remain at the sanctuary on the Day of Atonement. It was judgment day.

Let's now move 2300 years later, as the prophetic alarm clock counted down. According to this prophecy, starting in 457 B.C., the alarm bells sounded when the hands of time rested upon October 1844. At this moment the heavenly sanctuary was to be cleansed. It had huge implications for God's people, so we should expect that God would follow His own established pattern of bringing forth a new prophet to confirm that "the time is at hand"—as He did with Enoch and Noah, with Abram and Moses, and with Daniel and John the Baptist.

If He did, we should see that a prophet arose in or around the year 1844 proclaiming that the "Day of Atonement" had come, that the judgment of earth's inhabitants had come, and that God's people should "afflict their souls" in preparation.

Interestingly, history reveals that at least three people came upon the scene around the year 1844 claiming the mantle of God's messenger. And indeed, many more people arose claiming this role for themselves, but I want to focus on the three major players: the first is Joseph Smith; the second is Mary Baker; and the third is Ellen Harmon.

Joseph Smith was the founder of the Latter-day Saints, which has since grown into an international church organization. Did he proclaim the 2300-year prophecy set forth by Daniel? Did he call the attention of earth's inhabitants to God's judgment day? As the name of his church implies, they certainly believe in the coming of Christ, but there is no evidence that Smith proclaimed the fulfillment of Daniel 8:14 or even understood its tremendous importance.[4]

Our next candidate, Mary Baker, later Mary Baker Eddy, founded the Church of Christ, Scientist, later called Christian Science, in 1879. Upon close examination, Eddy also never touched upon God's message regarding the 2300-year prophecy.[5]

Since this prophetic period of history overflows with a significance that would naturally draw people to Christ, it stands to reason that the devil would do all in his power to muddy the waters of understanding with conflicting and false voices. And this period of history is indeed littered with innumerable people claiming to have the prophetic gift, with each supposedly carrying a message from God. Nearly every single one of them, however, failed to point people to the one vital message that God intended everyone to hear.

Except for Ellen Harmon, who later would become Ellen White. In her own words:

"At the age of eleven years I was converted, and when twelve years old was baptized, and joined the Methodist Church. At the age of thirteen I heard William Miller deliver his second course of lectures in Portland, Maine. I then felt that I was not holy, not ready to see Jesus. And when the invitation was given for church members and sinners to come forward for prayers, I embraced the first opportunity, for I knew that I must have a great work done for me to fit me for heaven. My soul was thirsting for full and free salvation, but knew not how to obtain it."[6]

The William Miller referred to by Ellen White was a Baptist preacher who had been led to study the prophecies in the book of Daniel that we've covered in this chapter. Miller assumed, incorrectly, as we shall see, that the Day of Atonement, the day on which the Jewish sanctuary was cleansed of sin, regarded Christ's second coming. He was "brought . . . to the solemn conclusion, that in about twenty-five years from that time [1818] all the affairs of our present state would be wound up."[7]

Miller determined that the earth itself was the sanctuary and that the cleansing meant that the planet would be purged by the fire of the second coming of Christ on October 22, 1844, a date he calculated through his study of Daniel. However, while he proposed what can be proven as an accurate date, his interpretation of the event—the second coming of

Jesus—was unfortunately in error. In an event that became known as the Millerites' Great Disappointment, October 23 dawned with no sign of Jesus. Hiram Edson, a follower of Miller, stated, "Our fondest hopes and expectations were blasted, and such a spirit of weeping came over us as I never experienced before. . . . We wept, and wept, till the day dawn."

Miller's mistake can be seen in the fact that he missed some important details in the sanctuary model and its services. He didn't recognize what the apostle Paul wrote about in Hebrews 8 and 9—that Christ, our high priest in heaven, had moved from the outer apartment of the sanctuary and entered into the Most Holy Apartment. This event was the Day of Atonement, the time for God's people to afflict their souls *in preparation* for Christ's second coming! "For on that day the priest shall make atonement for you, to cleanse you, that you may be clean from all your sins before the Lord" (Lev. 16:30).

Because the Millerites had missed this most significant detail, their faith in God would suffer a mighty trial.[8] But it was during this time of confusion and disappointment that God called Ellen Harmon to be His messenger. She would be His spokesperson, providing clarity and hope to the remaining flock of believers:

"From this time, up to December, 1844, my joys, trials, and disappointments were like those of my dear Advent friends around me. At this time I visited one of our Advent sisters, and in the morning we bowed around the family altar. It was not an exciting occasion, and there were but five of us present, all women. While I was praying, the power of God came upon me as I had never felt it before. I was wrapped in a vision of God's glory, and seemed to be rising higher and higher from the earth, and was shown something of the travels of the Advent people to the Holy City."[9]

A short time later she would detail this vision:

"I turned to look for the Advent people in the world, but could not find them, when a voice said to me, 'Look again, and look a little higher.' At this I raised my eyes, and saw a straight and narrow path, cast up high above the world. On this path the Advent people were traveling to the city, which was at the farther end of the path. They had a bright light set up behind them at the beginning of the path which an angel told me was the midnight cry. This light shone all along the path and gave light for their feet so that they might not stumble. If they kept their eyes fixed on Jesus, who was just before them, leading them to the city, they were safe. But soon some grew weary, and they said the city was a great way off, and they expected to have entered it before. Then Jesus would encourage them by raising His glorious right arm, and from His arm came a light which waved over the Advent band, and they shouted, 'Alleluia!' Others rashly denied the light behind them and said that it was not God that had led them out so far. The light behind them went out, leaving their feet in perfect darkness, and they stumbled and lost sight of the mark, and of Jesus, and fell off the path down into the dark and wicked world below. Soon we heard the voice of God like many waters."[10]

As God has always done in history, when a prophetic moment was at hand, He raised up a prophet to call sinners to repentance and point them to the fulfillment of the prophecy. In order to call His children from danger to safety, God has always spoken "to the prophets and gave them many visions. [He] taught lessons through the prophets" (Hosea 12:10, GW).

The following counsels from Ellen G. White are indicative of why she was God's chosen messenger, whereas the likes of Joseph Smith and Mary Baker Eddy could not be. Unlike them, she focused on Daniel's prophecies and earth's final judgment at exactly the time we would expect to hear from one of God's prophets.

"Jesus is our Advocate, our High Priest, our Intercessor. Our position is like that of the Israelites on the day of Atonement. When the high priest entered the most holy place, representing the place where our High Priest is now pleading, and sprinkled the atoning blood upon the mercy seat, no propitiatory sacrifices were offered without. While the priest was interceding with God, every heart was to be bowed in contrition, pleading for the pardon of transgression."[11]

"The cleansing of the sanctuary was the last service performed by the high priest in the yearly round of ministration. It was the closing work of the atonement—a removal or putting away of sin from Israel. It prefigured the closing work in the ministration of our High Priest in heaven, in the removal or blotting out of the sins of His people, which are registered in the heavenly records. This service involves a work of investigation, a work of judgment; and it immediately precedes the coming of Christ in the clouds of heaven with power and great glory; for when He comes, every case has been decided."[12]

We should not miss what she was saying here. It's the whole point of this book! We are in the judgment hour of earth's history—when every life must pass through judgment prior to Christ's second coming. We must search our hearts and plead with God to separate us from our sins.

But there is a problem.

---

[1] Daniel 9:24-26. In Bible prophecy a day accounts for one year. So 69 weeks, with 7 days a week, equals 483 days. Using the principle of a day for a year in Bible prophecy, this translates to 483 years. See Numbers 14:34 and Ezekiel 4:6.

[2] "This is eternal life, that they may know You, the only true God, and Jesus Christ whom You have sent" (John 17:3).

[3] For greater detail on this must-know subject, I recommend the book *Altar Call,* by Roy Gane of Andrews University. The publisher is Diadem (October 26, 1999).

[4] On June 27, 1844, in Carthage, Illinois, an angry mob broke into a jail where Smith was being held. Using a gun that his followers had smuggled into the jail, Smith shot four attackers before falling out of a window. Hurt and lying on the ground, he was shot several times before dying.

[5] The only event of significance happening around 1844 in Eddy's life was the birth of her son George.

[6] Ellen G. White, *Early Writings* (Washington, D.C.: Review and Herald Pub. Assn., 1882), p. 11.

[7] William Miller, *Apology and Defense* (Boston: Joshua V. Himes), pp. 11, 12.

[8] Some estimate that the number of believers at that time was as high as 500,000, but after the day passed without the expected return of Christ, the number plummeted to about 5,000.

[9] E. G. White, *Early Writings,* p. 13.

[10] *Ibid.,* pp. 14, 15.

[11] Ellen G. White, in *Signs of the Times,* June 28, 1899.

[12] Ellen G. White, *The Great Controversy* (Mountain View, Calif.: Pacific Press Pub. Assn., 1911), p. 352.

Chapter 6

Devastating Consequences

Before becoming a Christian, I would often sing a song called "Purple Haze," by Jimi Hendrix, the lyrics of which were clearly psychedelic in nature, despite Hendrix's denials that the song had anything to do with drugs. I also loved to sing the song "Born to Be Wild," by the rock group Steppenwolf.

What a change it was in my life when I invited Christ into my heart. I began to prefer singing such hymns as "Come, Holy Spirit," and "Blessed Be the Tie That Binds."

The devil, on the other hand, was not happy with my newfound taste in music. His plan has always been to destroy us, and the more he can deface the image of God in the eyes of humanity—whether through music or drugs or improper relationships—the better it is for him. The more elevated our pain index, the happier he is.

Sin is the cause of this pain.

If God would allow our eyes to see every painful detail in the spiritual war that surrounds us, I imagine we would immediately crumple into the fetal position and beg to be hidden from the horror. Yet 24 hours a day, seven days a week, God sees the filth of this world parade before Him—whether the sin is done at high noon or in the cover of night. With the news covering murders, rapes, genocides, and wars every single day, we do see enough of the horror to know that the suffering caused by sin is rampant on the earth.

By its very nature, sin sets the direction of a life in opposition to God, utterly destroying lives, families, and churches in the process. There isn't one good thing that could be said about the effects of sin.

I once had lunch with a psychologist in the home of a longtime friend. During our discussion I asked him about the general mind-set of his patients and their treatment. He shared this profound insight: "Most of my patients have convinced themselves that if they separate from their problems, they will experience great loss in their lives."

This is not unlike how you and I are when it comes to sin. Be honest with yourself. Why do you keep on sinning even though you know it causes suffering? Why don't you trust God that sinning is the worst thing you could do?

The devil has been completely successful at creating the illusion that if you trust God 100 percent, you will be worse off—that you will suffer some sort of irreplaceable loss. It sounds much like the story of Adam and Eve, doesn't it? They were convinced that God was withholding something worthwhile to their happiness on that tree in the garden. This deception will never end as long as the devil lives. Just as his focus has been upon himself for centuries, he has enslaved us to his same kind of inward thinking.

Through the prophet Moses, God led Israel out of Egypt—out of slavery. Since all sin is slavery, the story of the exodus of slaves represents a wider effort on God's part to free people from the bondage of sin. In fact, our identity as Christians is perfectly illustrated by the exodus of the Jews.

Using the biblical term, we could say these slaves were *justified*— declared righteous—when God moved to rescue them. They could not have earned their own freedom. Prior to their leaving Egypt, God instructed the Jews to kill a lamb and mark their doorposts with the blood of the innocent creature. Everyone within the marked home was "under the blood of the lamb." When the destroying angel flew over these dwellings, he spared the inhabitants. Their acceptance of the blood of the lamb was their justification.

Next, the Jews soon found themselves at the edge of the Red Sea, with the army of Pharaoh in hot pursuit. Likewise, the devil never wants to let his captives go. He is always enraged when God plucks the prey from his grasp. He will stop at nothing to keep us in bondage. I discovered this fact the hard way.

While we were conducting a series of prophecy meetings in India, God gave our team great success. Standing on the banks of a muddy river, as the sun was in full bloom and cattle grazed nearby, I watched my pastor friend baptizing those who had come forward to accept Christ. These people had been led by the Creator out of the bondage of Hinduism, and the devil was furious!

The pastor was standing about waist-deep in the river as the next believer approached. She was a woman who, dripping wet, might have tipped the scales at 90 pounds; he, on the other hand, rippled with muscle and probably weighed at least 180 pounds. It was a joyous sight to behold, a new believer in Christ yearning for baptism.

Yet in the next moment, as she disappeared beneath the water, I realized something wasn't right. The pastor appeared to be in a desperate struggle. The woman wasn't coming up! The pastor struggled to lift her from the shallow depths; she could have drowned at any moment! But at last, with superhuman effort, the pastor pulled her up to safety.

Her body was grotesquely contorted, her arms twisted into what seemed an impossible shape. She appeared to be in great pain, but she wasn't making any sound. Although I had never been witness to this kind of thing before, God impressed me—it was demon possession!

I ran to the water's edge to help carry the woman to dry land. Without thinking, I grabbed hold of her with both hands and exclaimed, "In the name of Jesus Christ, I demand that you come out of this woman. You have no power over her. She is God's." Instantly the struggle was over; she was free. Her eyes focused as she wiped her dripping hair away from her face. She got up, looked around, and then walked up the grassy slope as if nothing had happened.

The devil had been furious. He had attempted to drown this new child of the King in the baptismal waters, but God would not have it. I can faithfully testify that God is far more powerful than the adversary; He is the same God today that led Israel to safety at the Red Sea.

Let's now return to the account of Exodus 14. Satan was preparing to hurl all of Egypt's military might against the slaves whom God dared to separate from his bondage. As 600 chariots moved swiftly across the barren ground toward their prey, the Jews experienced a crisis of belief. "It would have been better for us to serve the Egyptians than that we should die in the wilderness" (verse 12). They could not see past their immediate difficulty, even after they'd seen the plagues descend on the Egyptians.

It makes some sense. Here was a nation of simple slaves who for generations had been told what to do, when to do it, where to do it, and for how long. They didn't have an obvious escape route available, and even if they had had weapons, they wouldn't have had a clue as to how to use them against professional warriors. Now with water at their back and a destroying army at their front, who wouldn't be tempted to doubt God's plan in that moment?

But then the prophet stepped forward with a word from the Lord, "Do not be afraid. Stand still, and see the salvation of the Lord, which He will accomplish for you today. For the Egyptians whom you see today, you shall see again no more forever" (verse 13).

Suddenly a mighty cloud, something resembling a great pillar of fire, rose up between the children of Israel and the advancing army. Now it was time for Moses to lead the people from danger to safety. "Moses stretched out his hand over the sea; and the Lord caused the sea to go back by a strong east wind all that night, and made the sea into dry land, and the waters were divided" (verse 21).

Over the next few hours the people experienced something like a baptism as they walked through the dry waters prepared by their God. "The children of Israel went into the midst of the sea" (verse 22). Still, in his boundless fury, Satan marshaled his forces to pursue and trample the fleeing slaves. Yet God's people would witness another demonstration of His power to deliver those who follow Him.

The chariots brazenly advanced, clattering down the rocky bank and onto the seabed highway. The soldiers could smell victory; it was only a matter of minutes before they would humble this people and their God.

Except the Lord removed the restraints. Whatever power held the water at bay was loosed, and the highway was immediately covered in torrents of raging water. It was impossible for the soldiers to stay afloat while clothed in their full-battle attire. In moments the last of Egypt's mighty men lay at the bottom of the Red Sea.

Many skeptics, including professed Christians, doubt this epic account of history. Do you? If so, it just might speak volumes about the God you think you worship. It so happens that this was exactly Israel's problem: doubting the power of God and His mighty ability to save to the "uttermost" those who call upon Him. The Jews' lack of belief ultimately had devastating consequences, but for now they rejoiced over the destruction of the Egyptian army.

Next they would depart from the Red Sea, their baptism by water, and enter into a process known as "sanctification." This was to be a process of transformation, being changed from slaves of sinful Egypt to servants of a righteous God. It was time for them to learn about their real family, to be repatriated, as it were, and it was time for them to start relying upon God for all of their needs. That process was not an easy one for them, and it's often not an easy one for us.

Even with this amazing victory to add to their ever-growing accounts of God-sized miracles, they were full of complaints. They continually vented to Moses and Aaron their growing frustration of their desert journey: "Oh, that we had died by the hand of the Lord in the land of Egypt, when we sat by the pots of meat and when we ate bread to the full! For you have brought us out into this wilderness to kill this whole assembly with hunger" (Ex. 16:3).

This was Stockholm syndrome kicking in at full blast! And it's quite common in the Christian experience. After Christ has miraculously saved them, new Christians are pressed with doubts about their new identity and need for change in their lives. They often grumble about the things they must leave behind to become true servants of the Lord.

Yet despite the Jews' continual complaints and their desire to return to their former slave masters, God loved them. They were His chosen family, after all. It was time to lead them into the land flowing with milk and honey.[1]

Let us now jump forward to their account in Numbers 13, when the nation selected a few men to spy out the Promised Land. Forty days later the men were spotted coming back over the rise. I imagine the people shouting to each other the good news. Then a small child spots the returning men carrying something between them and asks, "What are they carrying?" Another shouts, "It's a cluster of grapes! It's so big that it takes two men to carry it!"

They had found heaven on earth! Everything that God had told them about this land was true. And He also told them that He had given them the land; it was literally theirs for the taking. They joyfully celebrated the good news as the spies gave their awesome account.

Unfortunately, all except two would quickly change their tune. One spy spoke up with fear in his voice and uttered one of the worst lines of faithlessness in the Bible: "Nevertheless the people who dwell in the land are strong" (verse 28). Satan and his legions must have rejoiced at these words when they began spreading through the entire camp.

Spurred on by the foolishness of one, many joined the sorrowful chorus: "We are not able to go up against the people, for they are stronger than we" (verse 31). Other spies added their pitiful assessment: "We saw the giants; . . . and we were like grasshoppers in our own sight" (verse 33).

It had devastating consequences for the slaves. I call them slaves because they would not allow God to raise them above their former existence and thereby enable them to enter into a new and joyful relationship with their Savior. They were at the borders of the Promised

Land. They only had to believe and receive—to walk in and take it—but they refused to act.

The next words blubbered out of their crying corporate mouth must have caused unimaginable pain to God:

"The congregation lifted up their voices and cried, and the people wept that night. And all the children of Israel complained against Moses and Aaron. . . . 'If only we had died in the land of Egypt! Or if only we had died in this wilderness! Why has the Lord brought us to this land to fall by the sword . . . ? Would it not be better for us to return to Egypt?'" (Num. 14:1-3).

Still, two faithful men attempted to turn the hearts of the people back toward God. They knew the Lord could and would deliver the giants into their hands. "We are well able to overcome it," shouted a confident Caleb (Num. 13:30). But it was too late; the slaves had already run to the open arms of the devil. They closed their ears from hearing the truth.

What was the truth? Yes, powerful giants, a mighty warring race, inhabited the land. Indeed, Og, the king of Bashan, spoken of several times in the Bible, might have tapped in at 12 feet, according to some theologians.[2] I know a little of what the Jews were feeling. I once found myself on a street in Washington, D.C., with an eight-foot guy angrily approaching me. I would have serious concerns about an entire nation of giants.

This skepticism of God's power to save resulted in a horrible tragedy. On that fateful day, as tears flowed down the cheeks of everyone contemplating facing those giants, as they looked hopelessly into that glorious land, God eventually granted the slaves their preference: to die in the wilderness.

The wish of everyone, that is, except the faithful—Moses, Aaron, Joshua, and Caleb. It's sad to think about. These were the faithful ones, yet they spent the next 40 years wandering in the desert because of the sins of the doubters, the ones who preferred slavery to freedom. The effects of sin have devastating consequences on not only the one who sins but also upon everyone around them. Yes. Sin is that bad.

Forty years later the children and grandchildren of the Egyptian slaves approached the borders of the Promised Land. In contrast to their doubting ancestors, this generation believed in the promises of their God.

Scouts were again dispatched to survey the land, and a few of these men targeted the walled city of Jericho. We'll pick up this thrilling narrative in Joshua 2, where we meet Rahab, a pagan prostitute. Her house of business was located near the city gate, a high-traffic area. It's likely that many men were coming and going day and night to her establishment; thus, it provided perfect cover for the spies. What's two more men visiting a prostitute's lair?

The men likely entered the city under the cover of darkness and soon made their way to the roof, where they intended to curl up for the night. But before they could close their eyes, Rahab appeared. She was troubled. She whispered to them,

"I know that the Lord has given you the land, *that the terror of you has fallen on us.* . . . For we have heard how the Lord dried up the water of the Red Sea for you when you came out of Egypt. . . . And as soon as we heard these things, *our hearts melted;* neither did there remain any more courage in anyone because of you, for the Lord your God, He is God in heaven above and on earth beneath" (verses 9-11).

This is an absolutely amazing moment. It's a statement of faith from the lips of a sinful prostitute of a people who were the enemy of God's people. Let's unpack her words and examine them closely. First, she confesses that terror has seized everyone in the country. They had their own spies who had been tracking the nomadic nation. They knew full well that this nomadic nation was gathering on the border of their homeland.

Why the terror? Because they remembered what had happened 40 years before. They'd heard about the mighty power of God to destroy an entire army. So when they saw the Jews at their borders, their hearts "melted" in hopeless fear. Can a warrior fight, even a giant, if his heart has been melted?

Let's not miss the irony either. This warrior nation of giants that had paralyzed and panicked Israel had itself been in utter fear at the approach of the Hebrew God 40 years earlier. While Israel was camped at the borders of the land flowing with milk and honey, the giants were having their own crisis of faith.

It's too bad Israel had such an "I" problem 40 years earlier. Their unfaithful spies focused their eyes on the giants and concerned themselves with their own weaknesses, while the giants had their focus on the God of heaven and His strength. How different the outcome could have been for Israel if they had only realized the biggest giant of all—God—was going to fight for them the entire time.

It's precisely the same idea with you and me. Satan wants you to focus on your weaknesses, your "impossible" situation, your giants—whatever they might be. But you plus God equals an unbeatable army. God had already given the Jews the land by promise. It was theirs. Likewise, God has already given us victory with the same sure promise.

Look at Joshua 1:3; it's an amazing promise given to Israel by God: "Every place that the sole of your foot will tread upon I have given you." Notice the words "will tread." They denote future action. Now, what about "have given"? They indicate past action. God told Israel He had already given them the land (past action), so all the Jews needed to do was trust God, move in, and set up house (future action).

Instead, they did nothing but worry, fret, cry, moan, complain, and gripe. Yet nothing they did made the situation better. This behavior never does. It's about what God can do, not about what we can't do. If we place our trust in God and follow Him, we will never go wrong!

Rahab saw the writing on the wall. She begged the spies to remember her and her family when God would eventually destroy Jericho. It seems as if the Holy Spirit had gone ahead of the spies to tutor this woman, because she boldly stated, "For the Lord your God, He is God in heaven above and on earth beneath" (Joshua 2:11).

In response to her faith, the men instructed the prostitute to hang a scarlet cord out of her window and bring all of her family members into the home when the battle began. Anyone who did not follow the instructions would be lost.

Think about that scarlet cord. Isn't it similar to when God instructed Israel to paint their doorposts with the lamb's blood? It is the only way for a family to be safe and secure from danger—when it resides under the redeeming blood of the Lamb. "Come now, and let us reason together. . . . Though your sins are like scarlet, they shall be as white as snow; though they are red like crimson, they shall be as wool" (Isa. 1:18).

Up to this time in Israel's history, their journey had been very bleak. Their actions had resulted in devastating consequences for everyone associated with them. But now, not only did Rahab's interaction with Israel save her family—she also became the great-great-grandmother of King David, whose direct descendant was Jesus! How great is that? What faith in God can do!

Maybe you've done things in your life of which you are deeply ashamed. Well, as the Master Potter, God is looking for clay willing to be fashioned into His own image. You can choose to be that clay no matter where you come from. He is ready to make you into a beautiful vessel to house the Holy Spirit, just as He did for the harlot Rahab.

Unfortunately, not everyone followed God's instructions, as Rahab did. God was very specific regarding the destruction of the city. The Israelite army was to march, shout, and take possession of the city, and then destroy everything except the gold, silver, brass, and iron, which were to be kept for the Lord's treasury. To keep anything for themselves, the Jewish people would bring down the wrath of God upon them.

After an incredibly successful war campaign, the nation was certainly ready for the next battle—but something went terribly wrong. They were beaten badly. When Joshua inquired of the Lord what had happened, he was told that someone had not followed His directions.

In the battle many men had died. The only reason was that someone transgressed a direct command of God. The entire nation had so much riding on this battle, so word spread rapidly and everyone wondered who dared to bring such devastation upon the camp.

The finger of blame eventually pointed at a man named Achan. Before the crowds, Joshua addressed the rebel, "I beg you, give glory to the Lord God of Israel, and make confession to Him, and tell me now what you have done; do not hide it from me" (Joshua 7:19). You probably could have heard a pin drop in those moments.

In short order Achan did confess: "Indeed I have sinned against the Lord. . . . When I saw among the spoils a beautiful Babylonian garment, two hundred shekels of silver, and a wedge of gold weighing fifty shekels, I coveted them and took them. And there they are, hidden in the earth in the midst of my tent, with the silver under it" (verses 20, 21).

Don't miss this point: Even in his confession, Achan revealed that his heart was still attached to the garments and precious metals. This attachment to sin had devastating consequences. While he might not have doubted God's ability to conquer giants, he refused to stay away from what God commanded the people to avoid. He didn't let go of the sin.

Men ran to Achan's tent to verify the story and, sure enough, the very items God had said to keep away from were the very items he hid in his home. Adam and Eve had let the devil tempt them into taking the forbidden fruit, and like that sad pair, Achan's family would pay for his sin.

"Joshua, and all Israel with him, took Achan the son of Zerah, the silver, the garment, the wedge of gold, his sons, his daughters, his oxen, his donkeys, his sheep, his tent, and all that he had, and they brought them to the Valley of Achor. And Joshua said, 'Why have you troubled us? The Lord will trouble you this day.' So all Israel stoned him with stones; and they burned them with fire after they had stoned them with stones" (verses 24, 25).

Achan faithlessly chose the things of this earth that perish, even though God had already promised him everything else; he desired the gold, silver, and the things of this world. He and his entire family and all they held dear were lost forever. In contrast, the pagan Rahab desired to become part of the family of God; her family and all they possessed were saved.

This is the story of the Christian's faith, isn't it? It doesn't matter where we come from; God will save anyone who comes to Him in faith. But they must also both obey Him and believe in His promises. They must grab hold of those promises. Otherwise, they fall into perilous sin.

And this sin causes tremendous pain and suffering that affects not only us but everyone else with whom we come in contact. The children of Israel, especially Achan, discovered just how dangerous sin can be.

That's why God is always trying to move us from danger to safety. The question is How is He going to do that for you today?

---

[1] "The Lord said: 'I have surely seen the oppression of My people who are in Egypt, and have heard their cry because of their taskmasters, for I know their sorrows. So I have come down to deliver them out of the hand of the Egyptians, and to bring them up from that land to a good and large land, to a land flowing with milk and honey'" (Ex. 3:7, 8).

[2] According to Guinness World Records, the tallest man still living, as of February 2011, was a mere 8.3 feet tall!

Chapter 7

From Danger to Safety, Part 2

For years I've had a beautiful painting hanging on the wall of my office. It depicts Christ overlooking Jerusalem. I love contemplating the wonderful message of love, warmth, and care the piece calls to mind. As Christ surveyed the city of peace, as tears flooded His eyes, He sighed, "O Jerusalem, Jerusalem . . . ! How often I wanted to gather your children together, as a hen gathers her chicks under her wings, but you were not willing!" (Matt. 23:37). Oh, how I long to be gathered under the wings of our great Protector and Provider.

It was only recently, however, that I realized an important part of this poignant scene had completely escaped me. For a very long time I never quoted the entire verse in a sermon. This, I'm convinced, made the devil happy. See if you agree with my reasoning.

In the desert wilderness Satan appeared to Jesus after He had completed a 40-day fast. Christ's mission was to save humanity, but the devil was determined to trip Him up. After tempting Jesus to turn stones to bread, Satan took Jesus to the pinnacle of the Temple in Jerusalem and quoted Scripture. "If You are the Son of God, throw Yourself down. For it is written: 'He shall give His angels charge over you,' and, 'In their hands they shall bear you up, lest you dash your foot against a stone'" (Matt. 4:6).

The devil is one of the greatest theologians on earth and is delighted to apply Scripture to suit his warped desires. When he quoted Psalm 91 to Jesus, he not only twisted the meaning, but omitted a very important part. Here is the entire quote, with my emphasis on the part he left out: "For He shall give His angels charge over you, *to keep you in all your ways*. In their hands they shall bear you up, lest you dash your foot against a stone" (verses 11, 12).

"To keep you in all your ways." The very portion that spoke to the mission of Christ regarding our salvation was left out! This has been the devil's method for ages—quote only a portion of a Bible verse to twist or conceal its true meaning.

In similar fashion I believe that I might have been deceived into leaving out the first half of Matthew 23:37: "O Jerusalem, Jerusalem, *the one who kills the prophets and stones those who are sent to her!* How often I wanted to gather your children together, as a hen gathers her chicks under her wings, but you were not willing!"

Doesn't omitting "the one who kills the prophets and stones those who are sent to her" leave out a crucial component of this verse? It tells us *why* Jerusalem was being judged in the first place!

Because sin placed a deadly barrier between deity and humanity, it wasn't long after the fall of man that God began using faithful men and women to speak on His behalf. Ever since, their day jobs have been to admonish, warn, direct, counsel, encourage, intercede, and instruct humankind—to call us out of sin so the Father can gather us under His mighty wings. True prophets always call people from danger to safety.

"And God said to Noah, 'The end of all flesh has come before Me, for the earth is filled with violence through them; and behold, I will destroy them with the earth'" (Gen. 6:13). In the 120 years that followed this message from God, Noah, by the witness of his actions and preaching, called for people to seek God's haven of safety.

Likewise, God counseled Israel not to follow the disgusting practices of the nations that surrounded them. A list of these evils is given in Deuteronomy 18:9-12 and includes witchcraft, fortunetelling, astrology, and attempting to speak with the dead, among others. Each loathsome act is a deceitful tool of the devil calculated to destroy those who engage in their folly.

Through the prophets, God has *always*—then and now—wanted to protect His people, to provide them with a solid foundation in spiritual matters so they would not be swayed by the wickedness around them. He gave them a tremendous gift, what the Bible calls the gift of prophecy, as recorded in the same chapter of Deuteronomy, "I will raise up for them a Prophet like you from among their brethren, and will put My words in His mouth, and He shall speak to them all that I command Him" (verse 18).

Many have argued that since we are living in the era of the Christian church, we have no need of prophets anymore, that God no longer works in the same way. But I submit to you that even in this late century, God continues to call us to His side in the same manner that He has done throughout history. His method has not changed. "I am the Lord, I do not change" (Mal. 3:6). In Him there is "no variation or shadow of turning" (James 1:17).

The prophet, speaking on behalf of God, is still one of His means of guiding us from danger to safety. Do you think a prophet is merely an Old Testament relic? Well, let's examine what the New Testament has to say about it:

"Do not believe every spirit, but test the spirits, whether they are of God; because many *false prophets* have gone out into the world" (1 John 4:1).

"He Himself gave some to be apostles, some prophets, . . . for the edifying of the body of Christ, till we all come to the unity of the faith and of the knowledge of the Son of God" (Eph. 4:11-13).

"Beware of *false prophets*, who come to you in sheep's clothing, but inwardly they are ravenous wolves" (Matt. 7:15).

I couldn't resist highlighting one of the things in these passages that jumped out at me. Again and again we are cautioned against accepting the words of *false prophets*.

Lots of moms tell their kids, "Don't hang around with that crowd; they're no good." Or "They are not the kind of people you should be associating with." What is the unsaid meaning of this counsel? You should make friends with the good kids!

Likewise, by implication, these Bible writers are telling us, "Don't hang around the false prophets; hang around the good ones!" Jesus adds another point of guidance about prophets in Matthew 7:20: "Therefore by their fruits you will know them." Simple enough: Bad prophets produce bad fruit, and good prophets produce good fruit. Even as a kid, I could tell who was bad by looking at a person's deeds. Likewise, if you want to find a real prophet of God, you need to be a fruit inspector!

Let's return to the subject of Ellen G. White. As I mentioned earlier, she came on the scene in 1844, the start of humanity's final judgment hour. How important was this event? Was it as important as Israel being called out of bondage from Egypt by Moses? How about the first coming of Christ, heralded by John the Baptist?

Indeed, the universe has been waiting 6,000 years for the final judgment hour and the second coming of Christ. This is a message of supreme importance! And as we already know, "Surely the Lord God does nothing, unless He reveals His secret to His servants the prophets" (Amos

3:7). The prophets have always been God's chosen vessels to reveal His plans to humanity. However, throughout history people have invented any and every excuse not to listen to His prophets.

The Lord says, "If you will not listen to Me, to walk in My law which I have set before you, to *heed the words of My servants the prophets whom I sent to you*, . . . then I will make this . . . city a curse to all the nations of the earth" (Jer. 26:4-6). God will not bless those who come up with excuses to ignore His messengers.

If, as we've discussed, Ellen White was one such messenger, used by God to guide us through the turbulent final hours of earth's history, shouldn't we listen to her counsel if we wish to prosper spiritually? "Believe in the Lord your God, and you shall be established; believe His prophets, and you shall prosper" (2 Chron. 20:20). Prospering is directly connected to believing in His messengers. This is especially relevant Bible teaching in an era of skeptics and nonbelief inside and outside of His church!

Remember Jesus overlooking Jerusalem? His sorrow was that the children of Israel could not prosper because they stoned and killed His prophets. It's utterly tragic! I imagine that most of them believed they had good cause to doubt, ignore, debase, or even kill those sent by God; they even came up with arguments to kill Jesus.

Of course, the devil is well aware that he has a much better chance of deceiving God's people if they do not heed the guidance and warnings sent to us by His prophets.

I know it's not the easiest thing to accept in this culture and time. Even my wife found it difficult to believe at first; she says, "The idea of a prophet was extremely foreign to my concept of contemporary thought and culture. Basically, it was unbelievable."

What changed her mind? She decided to follow Jesus' counsel and became a fruit inspector. And after she had thoroughly inspected the writings of Ellen White, her mind was opened and she was ready to listen.[1]

What kind of fruit did Ellen White produce? The scope of her writings and counsel number in the tens of thousands of pages—far too vast to be considered here.

"At the time of her death, Ellen White's literary productions totaled approximately 100,000 pages: 24 books in current circulation; two book manuscripts ready for publication; 5,000 periodical articles in the journals of the church; more than 200 tracts and pamphlets. . . . Compilations made after her death from Ellen White's writings bring the total number of books currently in print to more than 130."[2]

She had about 2,000 reported visions, which varied in length from less than a minute to nearly four hours. Regarding those visions, the trustees of the Ellen G. White Estate make this observation:

"The work of anyone who claims to bear God's message must meet the sure tests of the Word of God, such as 'by their fruits ye shall know them,' . . . the fulfillment of predictions, etc. While the physical phenomena that sometimes accompanied the visions do not rightfully form a test, they did supply, in the minds of most eyewitnesses, confirmatory evidence of the working of divine power. Those who personally witnessed Ellen White in vision observed very carefully what took place. From the eyewitness accounts available, we can build the following summary:

1. "Immediately preceding a vision, both Mrs. White and others in the room experienced a deep sense of the presence of God.
2. "As the vision began, Ellen White would exclaim, 'Glory!' or 'Glory to God!' at times repeated.
3. "She experienced a loss of physical strength.
4. "Subsequently, she often manifested supernatural strength.
5. "She did not breathe, but her heartbeat continued normally, and the color in her cheeks was natural.
6. "Occasionally she gave exclamations indicative of the scene being presented to her.
7. "Her eyes were open, not with a vacant stare, but as if she were intently watching something.
8. "Her position might vary. At times she was seated; at times reclining; at times she walked about the room and made graceful gestures as she spoke of matters presented.
9. "She was absolutely unconscious of what was occurring about her. She neither saw, heard, felt, nor perceived in any way her immediate surroundings or happenings.
10. "The close of the vision was indicated by a deep inhalation, followed in about a minute by another, and very soon her natural breathing resumed.
11. "Immediately after the vision, all seemed very dark to her.
12. "Within a short time she regained her natural strength and abilities."[3]

Some additional intriguing facts about Ellen White include:
- She is one of the most translated women writers in the history of literature.
- Just prior to the 1906 San Francisco earthquake, she said the city would face destruction.
- At a time when some doctors prescribed smoking as a treatment for lung disease, she said tobacco was a malignant poison.
- In the 1860s she wrote, "Cancer is a germ [virus]." Medical science had no idea that this was true until recent years.
- She warned that excessive X-rays could be dangerous.
- She saw that unrest and drug addiction among the youth of the world would be problematic.

Just a few visible fruits of her ministry, which has made a huge and positive impact upon the lives of millions of people around the world, include:

1. The church she helped to found, the Seventh-day Adventist Church, is one of the larger Christian denominations, with a presence in more than 200 countries.
2. Worldwide, the Seventh-day Adventist Church has established 173 hospitals, 381 clinics, 115 retirement centers, 36 children's homes, and dozens of schools and universities. It has also established 63 publishing houses and 17 literature ministry seminaries.
3. Seventh-day Adventists live longer than the general American population and suffer fewer diseases.[4]

The Adventist Church and her people are living proof of the truthfulness of the promise "Believe His prophets, and you shall prosper." That's why to help you both grow and prosper, I will be using Scripture and the counsel of Ellen White throughout the book. What she says about growing in faith and being free from sin will absolutely astound you and give you courage.

Of course, Satan does not want anyone in the church to prosper—you included—so it is critical that we base our faith on the Bible. And if we are to believe the Bible, we must believe in His prophets as well.

The following statements from Ellen White offer some background as to what has been going on with the battle for hearts and minds in the church today:

"Satan's purpose is . . . to make of none effect the testimonies of the

Spirit of God. If he can lead the minds of the people of God to see things in a perverted light, they will lose confidence in the messages God sends through His servants; then he can the more readily deceive, and not be detected."[5]

"It is Satan's special object to prevent this light from coming to the people of God, who so greatly need it amid the perils of these last days."[6]

"It is Satan's plan to weaken the faith of God's people in the *Testimonies*. Next follows skepticism in regard to the vital points of our faith, the pillars of our position, then doubt as to the Holy Scriptures, and then the downward march to perdition."[7]

Do you see the potential for disaster when we ignore a prophet of God? It is through the prophets that God calls you and me from danger to safety—to be protected under His mighty wings. We are on the precipice of eternity! Grasp all of God so you do not lose your balance!

Ellen White's counsel was given to us for such a time as this. And these are exciting times! God has great things in store for us—total freedom from sin. Let's see how.

---

[1] Regarding her reading of the book *Ellen G. White: Prophet of Destiny*, by Rene Noorbergen, my wife says, "As soon as I finished the book, I viewed her writings in a completely different way, with a changed attitude. The more I read her writings, the more it became clear to me that her messages had been given to her by God. I realized then that she was indeed a prophet."

[2] Facts obtained from the Ellen G. White Estate, Silver Spring, Maryland.

[3] www.whiteestate.org/issues/faq-egw.html.

[4] For additional study, I highly recommend Herbert E. Douglass, *Messenger of the Lord: The Prophetic Ministry of Ellen G. White* (Nampa, Idaho: Pacific Press Pub. Assn., 1998).

[5] Ellen G. White, *Manuscript Releases* (Silver Spring, Md.: Ellen G. White Estate, 1993), vol. 12, p. 201.

[6] Ellen G. White, *Testimonies for the Church* (Mountain View, Calif.: Pacific Press Pub. Assn., 1948), vol. 2, p. 608.

[7] *Ibid.*, vol. 4, p. 211.

Chapter 8

Breath—Bones to Life

The supermax Pelican Bay State Prison, located near Crescent City, California, was designed to keep in the worst of the worst. Inmates there are confined to an 8' x 10' cement cell for as much as 22 hours each day.

A man named Jim once resided behind the concrete walls of Pelican Bay. He was a muscled, tattooed-covered leader of a biker gang who had earned the privilege of being there with a rap sheet comprised of no less than 60 pages of various felonies and misdemeanors.

He was not one of society's nicest members. You certainly wouldn't have wanted him in your neighborhood or hanging around your family. But today he's warmly welcomed by families in church every weekend.

How could a transformation like this ever happen? The Holy Spirit traveled through those prison walls and melted his cold, angry heart. Jim now serves as a deacon in his local church. That's the power of Jesus Christ.

Every time I share Jim's story in a church, I receive a chorus of hearty amens coming from every corner of the building. But do you know what we don't often hear? We never hear shouts of praise for the person who's been in the church faithfully every week their whole lives, even if that person has a vibrant, living experience with Christ. Yet there should be! In this day and age, having a vibrant, living experience with Christ is a miracle.

The Lord is not the God of the spiritually dead; He is the Lord of the spiritually living! Our spiritual life is rooted in Him, sustained by Him, and flourishes to maturity through Him. Without Him we are dry bones.

When Ezekiel was shown in vision a field of dry, lifeless bones, God quizzed him, "Son of man, can these bones live?"

His only answer was "O Lord God, You know" (Eze. 37:3). He had no other answer for God, because *there is no other answer*. Only God can give life. Only God can raise the dead and surge blood into lifeless hearts.

The Lord then promised Ezekiel, "I will put sinews on you and bring flesh upon you, cover you with skin and put breath in you; and you shall live. Then you shall know that I am the Lord" (verse 6).

Ezekiel faithfully responded, " 'Come from the four winds, O breath, and breathe on these slain, that they may live.' So I prophesied as He commanded me, and breath came into them, and they lived, and stood upon their feet, an exceedingly great army" (verses 9, 10).

A vibrant, living army whose commander is Jesus Christ should be an army moving ever forward and beating down the gates of hell on its way to final victory. But at present the church is a sickly army because most of its members are dead men walking. They were supposed to have died in the baptismal waters, but they never rose in the power of Christ and have never allowed His transforming mind to fully possess them.

Now is the time for that kind of change in our lives.

And it can't come too soon. There is no doubt in my mind that the Lord is preparing His people for this change in preparation for His soon second coming! God is sounding the trumpet, calling His people to be ready. Are you prepared? Is your experience with God this year better than it was last year? Are you allowing Him full access to you?

It is time for the clear word of truth to be trumpeted from our rooftops. It's time to have Spirit-led people in our congregations rather than self-driven slaves to the world. Now is the time to witness the dry bones in our pews come to life!

A Laser Light

"[Jesus] urged upon men the necessity of prayer, repentance, confession, and the abandonment of sin."[1] In the church, we often talk about the first three items in this list—prayer, repentance, and confession—but we go to great lengths to omit the fourth. For most churchgoers, to even think about the total abandonment of sin in the context of this life seems absurd. Most Christians believe it to be impossible.

Charles Finney, who has been called the father of modern revivalism, said, "To persist in sin is not to abandon it."[2] But is not sinning—at all—a real possibility? To answer this question, we must understand what God has in mind and to forget what we have been taught.

In Hebrews 12:29 Paul writes, "Our God is a consuming fire." In Isaiah 4:4 we read that the Lord would wash away the filth of Jerusalem "by the spirit of burning." Isaiah also offers this interesting message: "I will turn my hand upon thee, and purely purge away thy dross, and take away all thy tin" (Isa.1:25, KJV). Not long ago I sent this particular text to a friend, who thought I had erred. He wrote, "You made a mistake. The word 'tin' is a typo and should read 'sin.'" But "tin" is what is found in the text. Still, my friend had the right idea.

Tin is not a precious metal. God's desire is to refine us, to purge us, from all impurity, from all sin, with holy fire until there remains only gold within us. Not tin—no sin—but gold.

Shortly after Israel had crossed through the Red Sea, God instructed Moses to go to the people to "consecrate them . . . and let them wash their clothes. And let them be ready for the third day. For on the third day the Lord will come down upon Mount Sinai in the sight of all the people" (Ex. 19:10, 11). Here's the account of God's descent upon that mountain:

"There were thunderings and lightnings, and a thick cloud on the mountain; and the sound of the trumpet was very loud, so that all the people who were in the camp trembled. . . . Now Mount Sinai was completely in smoke, because the Lord descended upon it in fire. Its smoke ascended like the smoke of a furnace, and the whole mountain quaked greatly" Ex. 19:16-18). "The sight of the glory of the Lord was like a consuming fire on the top of the mountain in the eyes of the children of Israel" (Ex. 24:17).

Never before had a human been witness to such a display of pyrotechnics. The demonstration was so awesome that the phrase "the people who were in the camp trembled" is likely a big understatement!

Malachi may have looked upon this very scene when posing his question: "Who can endure the day of His coming? And who can stand when He appears? For He is like a refiner's fire and like launderers' soap" (Mal. 3:2). King David, writing in Psalm 24, answers Malachi's question this way: "He who has clean hands and a pure heart" (verse 4).

God had directed Moses to sanctify the people, which meant their eyes were to move from the worldly to the divine. They were to humble themselves and put away all sin. This experience was a prologue to Israel's future, a preview of the sanctuary and the Day of Atonement. They were to "afflict their souls" before God (Lev. 16:29). This same need applies to all of us living in these last moments of time, during earth's great day of atonement.

The Jews were to search their hearts to ensure they were right with God. There was to be sorrow for sin, a full confession, full repentance, and a turning away from evil. They were also to physically bathe themselves and clean their homes. If they did not follow these instructions fully, they were cut off from the camp.

God was teaching His children, this band of former slaves, that any and all sin has the power to separate and to destroy. His desire was to protect them and to be with them, and sin and God cannot exist in the same space. God "is a consuming fire" of sin, which means if anyone is attached to sin, or clings to it, they will eventually be consumed by God's fire.

The flip side, of course, is that "in all who submit to His power the Spirit of God will consume sin."[3] That's a wonderful promise! Yet Ellen White goes on to write, "But if men cling to sin, they become identified with it. Then the glory of God, which destroys sin, must destroy them."[4] "The glory of His countenance, which to the righteous is life, will be to the wicked a consuming fire."[5] By our freewill choice, God will burn out sin and separate it from the sinner—or He will burn up sin and the sinner who clings to it.

As King David wrote, only those with clean hands and pure hearts can survive God's fire. And Ellen White wrote, "The wicked are blotted from the face of the whole earth—consumed with the spirit of His mouth and destroyed by the brightness of His glory."[6]

Imagine that God owns a laser light with 100 trillion candlepower. He knocks on your door, and you answer. He explains, "The light I have is so bright that it immediately vaporizes sin. If you will invite Me into your home, I will do a room-by-room search and eradicate sin anywhere I find it. When I'm finished, your home will be as clean as new-fallen snow."

You decide to invite Him in, and He immediately begins His work of housecleaning. But when He reaches the master bedroom, you say, "God, this room is off-limits." You see, you have a few precious sins stored in there, and you would rather God just leave the door closed so everything in there can remain undisturbed. Surely God understands how hard it is, right?

Now, fast-forward to the Second Coming. Like the laser light, God's fire is so powerful that it will vaporize every sin it comes in contact with. If you had allowed God to do His scrubbing work in every room of your life, you would stand unharmed in the fire of His presence on the day of His appearing. But because you didn't let Him in the master bedroom to remove those precious sins with His surgically precise laser light, when He appears, you will be wholly destroyed along with those sins. They have become intertwined with your being, and where God is, sin cannot exist. There is no reason for you to make that ghastly mistake! You can choose which beginning—or ending—is yours.

Go and Sin No More?

To have an incorrect understanding of the seriousness of sin and Christ's desire to remove it from your life can be very hazardous to your eternity. It should come as no surprise that God wants you to be completely separated from sin right now. The Father loves you so much that He cannot stand leaving you to wallow in sin. That's why He will, with your permission, enter your home in an effort to re-create you—to completely remodel your home.

If you had the power to remove pain and heartache from a child or another loved one in your life, would you withhold that help? Of course not! Well, neither will our Father when it comes to the destructive power of sin. Does God really expect you to be free from sin? Let's examine the lessons of Jesus found in John 5. Through this story we'll see what His ultimate desire for us truly is.

A pitiful man had been lying at the Pool of Bethesda, hoping against all hope for some measure of healing. He was utterly paralyzed and had been suffering for 38 miserable years. Sadly, it was a case of "supreme wretchedness. . . . His disease was in a great degree the result of his own sin, and was looked upon as a judgment from God. Alone and friendless, [he felt] that he was shut out from God's mercy."[7]

On their own, sickness and suffering are hard to deal with, but when you know that the pain and trouble you are going through have been caused by your own wrong choices, it magnifies the heartache. But this sad situation offers hope and courage, because Jesus' compassion and forgiveness for the foolhardy still runs deep and wide. Ellen White describes the scene this way:

"The sick man was lying on his mat, and occasionally lifting his head to gaze at the pool, when a tender, compassionate face bent over him, and the words, 'Wilt thou be made whole?' arrested his attention. Hope came to his heart. He felt that in some way he was to have help. But the glow of encouragement soon faded. He remembered how often he had tried to reach the pool, and now he had little prospect of living till it should again be troubled. He turned away wearily, saying, 'Sir, I have no man, when the water is troubled, to put me into the pool: but while I am coming, another steppeth down before me.' Jesus does not ask this sufferer to exercise faith in Him. He simply says, 'Rise, take up thy bed, and walk.' "[8]

Complete and utter joy surely surged through every fiber of this man's being. He had been set free! The chains of sin and circumstance that had bound His body for so long were finally broken. I can imagine him celebrating—jumping and skipping along the paving stones of Jerusalem. With an overflowing heart he took a thank offering to the temple of God.

Leaving the pool area, Jesus soon joined the worshippers at the Temple and, as divine destiny would have it, He and the former paralytic came face to face again. But the tone in the Savior's voice was different. "See, you have been made well. Sin no more, lest a worse thing come upon you" (John 5:14). The seriousness in Jesus' demeanor left no doubt in the mind of the healed man: Jesus actually meant what He said.

But do you believe what Jesus said? Does the church? Or do we say, "Christ really wasn't expecting us to take this statement seriously"? Well, I suggest that this statement is an exclamation point that cries out, "Stop, sit up, and take notice!"

Let's examine another encounter recorded by John, the story of a prostitute taken in adultery, which emphasizes the lesson we've already learned, leaving us no room for doubt. The law called for stoning the prostitute to death, but Jesus took another route.

As John 8 records, Jesus was ministering to others in the Temple when church leaders set a trap for Him by throwing an adulterer, who had been caught in the act, down on the pavement in front of Him. They demanded that He pronounce sentence upon her.

With their rocks held high in the air, they waited for His response. The place was thick with tension and anticipation as Jesus lowered Himself to the level of the trembling woman. He then began to write something in the dust of the street.

The accusers drew nearer to read those words and discovered, to their great horror, that Jesus had been writing their personal sins for the world to see. As each pair of eyes traced their own wretchedness, the rocks once destined to carry out judgment slipped harmlessly to the ground. Silently the wayward church leaders slithered away to the darkest corners of the city.

Jesus now turned His loving focus to the woman of the night and said, "'Woman, where are those accusers of yours? Has no one condemned you?' She said, 'No one, Lord.' And Jesus said to her, 'Neither do I condemn you'" (verses 10, 11).

Moments before, her fate had seemed sealed; she had been preparing for the rocks to slam against her fragile body. Except, suddenly, the one some had called Messiah stepped in to forgive her. Could it really be? She had been saved from the clutches of death. Her heart raced with joy!

But Jesus was not finished. He spoke, "Go and sin no more. . . . I am the light of the world. He who follows Me shall not walk in darkness, but have the light of life" (verses 11, 12).

The power in the actions and words of Jesus was evident in the life of Mary of Bethany. *The Desire of Ages* records:

"Mary had been looked upon as a great sinner, but Christ knew the circumstances that had shaped her life. He might have extinguished every spark of hope in her soul, but He did not. It was He who had lifted her from despair and ruin. . . . In His strength she had overcome. . . . When to human eyes her case appeared hopeless, Christ saw in Mary capabilities for good. He saw the better traits of her character. The plan of redemption has invested humanity with great possibilities, and in Mary these possibilities were to be realized. Through His grace she became a partaker of the divine nature. The one who had fallen, and whose mind had been a habitation of demons, was brought very near to the Savior in fellowship."[9]

God wants to draw as near to you as He drew to Mary. We must comprehend that God wants to save us *from* our sins, not *in* our sins, so that we can live a vibrant life. But how?

Can you walk with the Light of the world and still have darkness within you? The prophet Amos asked a similar question: "Can two walk together, unless they are agreed?" (Amos 3:3). According to Jesus, it's impossible: "No one can serve two masters; . . . or else he will be loyal to the one and despise the other" (Matt. 6:24).

Jesus was serious. "Go and sin no more" was a life-or-death matter not only for the paralytic and the prostitute, but also for you and me. We cannot keep sinning. But before you faint with panic over that statement, realize that "whatever is to be done at His command may be accomplished in His strength. All His biddings are enablings."[10] Remember, it's all about what God can do through you when you give Him everything.

A Spiritual Defect

Our heavenly Father is a loving parent who desires to make us whole again and to put us back in harmony with the sin-free beings of His creation. Who plays the most important role in this sin-removal process? "It is the will of God to cleanse us from sin, to make us His children, and to enable us to live a holy life."[11]

If you answered "God," you're correct! Of course, you do have a major role to play in your own salvation, and we'll get to that soon. But make no mistake: God wants you to stop sinning, and the sooner you do, the better—and He will do most of the heavy lifting:

- to cleanse us from sin
- to make us His children
- to enable us to live a holy life

Moreover, the power of Christ that saves us is also the power that sustains us on the new sinless pathway. "Christ always separates the contrite soul from sin. He came to destroy the works of the devil, and He has made provision that the Holy Spirit shall be imparted to every repentant soul, *to keep him from sinning*."[12]

And thus we come back to God's promise in Eden to "put enmity" between us and the will of Satan. We are helpless without the all-powerful Creator dwelling in us; His indwelling Spirit is where the "overcoming" comes from. There isn't one shred of strength naturally residing in our sin-soaked bodies. We must have God living on the inside to repel sin—to keep us, like Moses, from being attracted to "passing pleasures of sin" (Heb. 11:25).

"No conversion is genuine which does not change both the character and the conduct of those who accept the truth. The truth . . . purifieth the soul."[13] You cannot have one without the other; no change in your life means no genuine conversion experience. Beyond that, you must experience ongoing conversion every day.

Here is another beautiful promise: "It is His [God's] purpose that the highest influence in the universe, emanating from the source of all power, shall be theirs [yours and mine]. They [we] are to have power to resist evil, power that neither earth, nor death, nor hell, can master, power that will enable them [us] to overcome as Christ overcame."[14] Add to this another remarkable promise found in the book *Christ's Object Lessons*: "As the will of man cooperates with the will of God, it becomes omnipotent."[15]

Wow! This is the power we must tap into. God is not the source of *some* power; He is the source of *all* power and, according to this promise, it is available to us so we will be enabled to "go and sin no more." Write down this formula and take it with you wherever you go . . .

The will of man
+ WILL of GOD
= *ONE* OMNIPOTENT WILL!

Hence, the shepherd's prayer in Psalm 23:3 becomes a "boots-on-the-ground" experience for us: "He leads me in the paths of righteousness for His name's sake." He doesn't want you to wander on the old paths that lead to sin, because you now carry the name of royalty—Jesus Christ. What we do now reflects upon our King and His court. It is time for us to graze where the Shepherd wants us to graze: in the fields of righteousness. When His will becomes your will, you will be happy and content to feast only at His table.

God is in the business of *complete* soul restoration. Jesus came not only to die for us, but also to provide us with a living and victorious example to follow.

"To him who overcomes I will grant to sit with Me on My throne, *as I also overcame* and sat down with My Father on His throne" (Rev. 3:21). What an amazing promise! Those who overcome sin are going to sit with Jesus on His throne as coregents. It really is beyond imagination! The very race of people who spat in God's face, who have given Him thousands of years of grief, and even killed His Son, will sit with Him as royalty.

To lay hold of this promise, we must allow Him to address our sin problem. This is what Jesus sought to reveal to Nicodemus, but, as so many are, he was deaf to spiritual truth, even though he himself was a theologian.

In John 3 we join this story as Nicodemus plies Jesus with pleasantries but avoids getting into topics of eternal importance. When it comes to everlasting life, however, humanity has no time to waste on superficial things, so Jesus cut to the chase, saying, "Unless one is born again, he cannot see the kingdom of God" (verse 3).

Bam! Right to the heart. It's not how great a theologian you are, but whether or not you allow self to die so God can live within you. Because of a defect in our spirits, we need a do-over. It is so important that Jesus told Nicodemus three times, "You must be born again." Ellen White expounds on this idea, writing, "Self-esteem and self-sufficiency are killing spiritual life. Self is lifted up; self is talked about. Oh, that self might die! 'I die daily,' said the apostle Paul. When this proud, boasting self-sufficiency and this complacent self-righteousness permeate the soul, there is no room for Jesus. He is given an inferior place, while self swells into importance and fills the whole temple of the soul. This is the reason why the Lord can do so little for us."[16]

God is in the business of taking hopelessness and turning it into hope, but we must agree to die to self. He has a way to eliminate the spiritual defect in you, but you must die to self so He can prepare you for the miraculous rebirth experience that will transform you into His image.

"No man receives holiness as a birthright, or as a gift from any other human being. Holiness is the gift of God through Christ. Those who receive the Savior become sons of God. They are His spiritual children, born again, renewed in righteousness and true holiness. Their minds are changed. With clearer vision they behold eternal realities. They are adopted into God's family, and they become conformed to His likeness, changed by His Spirit from glory to glory. From cherishing supreme love for self, they come to cherish supreme love for God and for Christ."[17]

The joy of transformation is waiting for you. All of heaven is waiting to pour out a blessing upon you that is far beyond your imagination!

---

[1] Ellen G. White, *Counsels to Parents, Teachers, and Students* (Mountain View, Calif.: Pacific Press Pub. Assn., 1913), p. 29.

[2] Barry Hankins, *The Second Great Awakening and the Transcendentalists* (Westport, Conn.: Greenwood Press, 2004).

[3] Ellen G. White, *The Desire of Ages* (Mountain View, Calif.: Pacific Press Pub. Assn., 1898), p. 107.

[4] *Ibid.*

[5] *Ibid.*, p. 600.

[6] E. G. White, *The Great Controversy*, p. 657.

[7] E. G. White, *The Desire of Ages*, p. 202.

[8] *Ibid.*

[9] *Ibid.*, p. 568.

[10] Ellen G. White, *Christ's Object Lessons* (Washington, D.C.: Review and Herald Pub. Assn., 1900), p. 333.

[11] Ellen G. White, *Steps to Christ* (Mountain View, Calif.: Pacific Press Pub. Assn., 1956), p. 51.

[12] E. G. White, *The Desire of Ages*, p. 311. (Italics supplied.)

[13] Ellen G. White, *Sons and Daughters of God* (Washington, D.C.: Review and Herald Pub. Assn., 1955), p. 288.

[14] E. G. White, *The Desire of Ages*, pp. 679, 680.

[15] E. G. White, *Christ's Object Lessons*, p. 333.

[16] Ellen G. White, *Lift Him Up* (Hagerstown, Md.: Review and Herald Pub. Assn., 1988), p. 310.

[17] Ellen G. White, in *Signs of the Times*, Dec. 17, 1902.

Chapter 9

Transformed

The apostle Paul recognized the pathway to overcoming sin.

In the book of Romans we find three chapters that deal with the idea of justification, the idea that Jesus places on us His righteous robe so that we might be seen as innocent in the eyes of God.

However, more than six chapters deal with the idea of sanctification, or the continual changes that must take place inside the believer, transforming our old hearts of stone into hearts of new flesh. Both justification and sanctification are the results of God's power and grace, but the process of our salvation from sin does not end at justification.

I believe Paul spends so much time discussing sanctification because God wants His people to understand the importance of the process. Remember, Paul is writing to a church of believers, reminding them that sin is a serious affront to God that doesn't go away simply because we're Christians. Paul *knew* that we must be set free of the old person: "Having been set free from sin, you became slaves of righteousness" (Rom. 6:18).

Romans 12:2 is a passionate summation of Paul's burden for his readers. "Do not be conformed to this world, but be transformed by the renewing of your mind." The Greek word translated as "transformed" is *metamorphoō*. It's an active verb that means to change into another form. It's where we get the word "metamorphosis," a major transformation of an organism, such as a caterpillar turning into a butterfly.

I wonder if Paul was thinking of the butterfly when he wrote this passage. I like to imagine that every day, on his way to the town square in Ephesus to preach the gospel, he paused near a small pond to check on a little caterpillar he'd happened to see one day as he prayed. At the time the little creature seemed to be preparing for something special as it fashioned some sort of attachment to a twig. Then a little while later a skinlike sheath began to form over its tiny body.

Paul was always in prayer for his flock in Ephesus, knowing they needed strength to continue in the faith they were called to follow. As he prayed one day, the cocoon began to wiggle. All of a sudden a tiny head poked out of the capsule—of a creature that had experienced an amazing *metamorphoō*. The once-tiny land-dwelling caterpillar had become a beautiful butterfly. Paul was ecstatic, having witnessed creation's perfect illustration of the growth and change that must occur in the Christian life. He then watched as the emerging butterfly opened two glorious wings to dry them in the warmth of the Mediterranean sun. After a brief pause, it then effortlessly negotiated the gentle breeze and headed skyward.

This is the experience God has in store for you. We have no strength to change ourselves, but the Creator has the desire and the re-creative power to make us new creatures. Our job is to allow Him to work this miracle inside us.

Do you believe that you're too bad of a person for God to change? Do you think you're hopelessly lost in temptation and sin? Ponder this: "None are so vile, none have fallen so low, as to be beyond the working of this power. In all who will submit themselves to the Holy Spirit a new principle of life is to be implanted; the lost image of God is to be restored in humanity."[1]

Which would you rather be—a worm chained to the earth or a butterfly soaring the lofty heights? I would be surprised if you chose the former, but the latter choice means you must play an active role in the life-changing process.

Are you in doubt that the Creator is a God of power who can transform a life—even yours? The following will boost your faith.

The Very Same God

Jesus broke up funerals by raising the dead. He is still breaking up funerals!

Her piercing cry brought me to an abrupt halt in the middle of my sermon. Seconds later she stood before me, a little child limply draped across her cradling arms. Fear contorted her face as she cried out in a language I did not understand. Eyes rolled back into his head, the young boy appeared to be dead.

I called for my friend James, a doctor, who was standing offstage. A wailing chorus pierced the muggy night air. As word spread throughout the crowd of the poor child's fate, I hoped James could help

Collecting my thoughts, I said to the crowd, "The devil does not want you to hear my message. But God is more powerful than the devil; let us go to Him in prayer and seek His help for the child." While I spoke with confidence, I was still thinking, *The child looks dead!*

I prayed aloud in earnest, asking God for healing and to stop Satan's disruption. Each time the translator would begin speaking, I glanced over at the doctor to see what was happening. At first he gave me a thumbs-down. So I kept praying. Still nothing. It was getting desperate, so I kept praying in earnest. Finally, a thumbs-up from James! I saw big smiles and heard huge sighs of relief. The crowd then gave praise to the Creator. That night these words traveled across the Hindu city in India, "There is a God who has power unlike other gods."

As I said the last prayer that night and the crowd left for their homes, that mother and child were uppermost on my mind. I shot a question to James that burned in my heart: "Was the child dead? What really happened tonight?"

"I don't know," he confessed. "I'm not sure."

"You're the doctor, James," I shot back.

"Yes, I am," he said. "And I just don't know . . . but there was no pulse."

We grappled over the evening's events that night, not willing to admit openly that perhaps God had actually raised the child from the dead, just as He had raised Lazarus.

A few years later I joined a group of pastors for lunch, and among them was Bob, a church leader. As we visited, Bob spoke of the night in India when he came to that very meeting years ago, the night the woman brought a dead child center stage. There he recounted, with incredible detail, that night to the other pastors at the table, leaving no doubt in their minds that the child was raised from the dead. Memories rushed back. It was and still is hard for me to comprehend the events of that incredible evening in India.

Does God still perform miracles? Well, the Bible says that as we get closer to the Second Coming, the devil will perform incredible signs in order to deceive humanity. But there will also be miracles from God meant to build up His work and to give glory to His name. God is still a God of miracles, and I believe He was that night in India. And I also believe that if He can do that, He can also free people from sin and the bondage of death!

Not an Isolated Incident

Shortly before I had arrived in Bangladesh on a mission trip, a young Christian man received a dream from God.

As he traveled to another large city on business, he dreamed that he should not tarry on the trip, as was his custom. Once there, he had an overwhelming sense that he must return home. His journey back took him past his mother's house in another village. He stopped for a visit, but when she offered him a meal, he felt impressed to continue on immediately.

Passing through another village, he spotted a large crowd near a pond. He drew closer and found a young boy lying on the bank. "What's wrong?" he asked.

"He's dead," someone answered. "Two hours ago we pulled him from the lake, and the doctor said he is dead." The crowd was made up largely of Hindus.

The young man later explained that he didn't know why, but he asked someone in the crowd to fetch him some hot mustard oil. He poured the oil on the lifeless form and began to massage the body while praying to God. Two more hours passed and the doctor, once again, examined the body. He again reported, "He is dead. Why do you continue?"

But then, after another two hours of prayer and massage, the boy coughed and suddenly sat up! Word of the miracle spread rapidly from village to village, and it wasn't long before two Hindu villages were worshipping Jesus, the one who gives life to the dead.

Five Witnesses

While in Ethiopia to film the TV series *Making Waves*, we began a search for a former fortuneteller who had quit the profession after discovering Jesus through our radio broadcasts. We traveled the dusty roads west of Addis Abba for hours, finally arriving at a farming village in the middle of nowhere.

I soon discovered that the story was much bigger than we had first been told. A villager discovered our radio program and told his brother, who also tuned in and began to share it with others. One of those people he told was the village fortuneteller of 42 years. Soon he and dozens of others accepted the Lord. At the same time another neighbor, a former prisoner, couldn't wait to get home and tell everyone he had found Christ through the airwaves.

These people had no pastor to guide them, but they continued to find spiritual nourishment from the daily radio programs and soon decided to form a worship group.

During this time the wife of the now ex-fortuneteller died. While alive, she hadn't wanted anything to do with God, because she missed the money from fortunetelling. After her death the new Christian believers were moved to pray for her.

With cameras rolling, I interviewed five villagers who had participated in that prayer vigil. "Are you sure she was dead?" I asked. "Our viewers might not believe it." Yes, all five were in complete agreement: She was dead! And after three days God raised her to life.

In that isolated village there was no help, no one to turn to in their time of need. But when they prayed asking God for help, He answered by filling that woman's dry, dead bones with the breath of His Spirit. Not surprisingly, she is now a part of the family of Christ!

Abide in Me, and I in You

I have often wondered why I can't perform such miracles on cue. But as Max Lucado once wrote, "It's not about me. It's all about God!" This fundamental truth provides perspective on why we don't see more mighty works of His Spirit in the church today. Can God trust us with the Holy Spirit and His miracle-working power? The church has an abundance of members and machinery, but do we have the transforming power of the Spirit? Most of our churches in North America are air-conditioned. But are they prayer-conditioned?

The working of miracles flows out of a God-focused relationship, not the other way around. The Bible is very plain: "This is eternal life, that they may *know* You . . . and Jesus Christ whom You have sent" (John 17:3). This is as real as it gets. Only the ones who *know* God deeply and surrender to His transforming presence can be trusted to handle this miracle power. Are you trustworthy?

On the flip side, some church members will appear before God on judgment day saying, " 'Lord, Lord, have we not prophesied in Your name, cast out demons . . . , and done many wonders in Your name?' And then I will declare to them, 'I never knew you; depart from Me, you who practice lawlessness' " (Matt. 7:22, 23). Working miracles is not proof of spirituality; what counts is whether one lives a transformed life free from lawlessness— from sin! God will know us because we act according to His righteousness.

So how can we be part of this miracle power? "We have now the invitations of mercy to become vessels unto honor, and then we need not worry about the latter rain; all we have to do is to keep the vessel clean and right side up and prepared for the reception of the heavenly rain, and keep praying, 'Let the latter rain come into my vessel.' "[2]

Our role is to say, "Lord, make me willing to be made willing. Transform me from a worm to a butterfly. Fill me with Your love. I am incapable of loving the way I must love. I am incapable of being what You want me to be. But You are the God of all power. Change me, mold me, make me, and shape me into Your image."

We must be ready "for the Promise," the fire of Pentecost (Acts 1:4). The apostle Peter and 119 other believers spent 10 days coming together, confessing their sins, and seeking God with all of their hearts, allowing God to "clean the cup" of their lives and making sure it was right side up, ready for the outpouring of the Holy Spirit (see Matt. 23:25, 26; Luke 11:39).

The great desire of our Lord is to transform us through the direct application of seven words of awesome power. They are "Abide in Me, and I in you" (John 15:4).

Miracles happen when God resides in His people. When the fire of Pentecost fell upon Peter, the unschooled fisherman preached with heavenly power and eloquence. Soon afterward he and John were climbing the Temple steps and found a man who had not walked since birth. Peter said, "Silver and gold I do not have, but what I do have I give you: In the name of Jesus Christ of Nazareth, rise up and walk" (see Acts 3:1-7). Peter extended his hand to the man, lifted him up, and he walked. That's power!

Peter had no earthly wealth, but he offered what he had—the indwelling presence of God. There are times I have plenty of silver and gold but not enough of the Holy Spirit, the power I need to be transformed and to bless those with whom I come in contact. How is your gold and silver supply in comparison to your supply of the Holy Spirit? God wants us to become the channels through which He can bless the world through exemplary lives.

What would happen if we determined to become the best friends Jesus ever had? What if we spent more time in prayer and study and pleaded for the outpouring of the Holy Spirit every day of our lives? Would we witness real miracles of healing? Or, better yet, the greatest miracle of all—to be raised from spiritual death, raising those of us who sit in the pews every week but are really not alive.

Father, please raise us up!

---

[1] E. G. White, *Christ's Object Lessons*, p. 96.

[2] Ellen G. White, *Manuscript Releases* (Silver Spring, Md.: Ellen G. White Estate, 1990), vol. 3, p. 414.

Chapter 10

A Wonderful Mind

The spiritual defect within each and every human being is a completely human-generated tragedy. This imperfection, which is centered in the mind, was the result of Adam's and Eve's choice to surrender their perfect minds to another power. This imperfection has since been handed down to every generation.

This is one reason we must be born again—to get a new mind; the old one is flawed and incapable of getting us into the kingdom. That's why God has a new mind ready for transplant into anyone who chooses to undergo the transformation process. But what is this new mind made from? One of the best descriptions of the new mind is found in Philippians 2.

The apostle Paul begins the chapter by exhorting the saints to have one mind, a mind guided by love. We know immediately from that description that he is not speaking of the spiritually defective mind. The mind he writes about values others above self.

In verse 5 Paul names the stunning source of this new mind: "Let this mind be in you which was also in Christ Jesus." Wow! The mind we're offered is the very mind of God! The passage that follows offers a detailed look into the workings of God's mind. It is Paul's completely convincing attempt to persuade us to leave our old minds behind for the new one.

Verse 6 begins this description by employing a literary device known as a chiastic structure. *Chi* is the Greek letter X. The Hebrews commonly used this device to focus on an idea of particular importance or to develop a certain pattern of thought. Paul uses the chiastic structure here to portray two unbelievable aspects of the mind of God. The first portrays Michael, before He left heaven, removing His kingly robes and stepping earthward as Jesus to "save His people *from* their sins" (Matt. 1:21). The second picture that comes into view, beginning in Philippians 2:9, is that of the Father pouring out His love to Jesus, restoring His prehuman glory, and, ultimately, allowing those who follow in His footsteps to share in that glory.

He will bestow the highest honor ever given to a created being, the honor of sitting with God on His throne (see Rev. 3:21).

Below, I've illustrated what occurred in the life of Christ, from verse 6 through 11, within the chiastic structure. As you follow along, you'll see the path Christ took in His descent to earth and, ultimately, the cross.

Emptied self	Full glory restored
Became a man	Every tongue confesses
Became a servant	Every knee should bow
Obedient to death	Name above every name
Death on the cross	Highly exalted Jesus

On the left side, you see the downward steps Jesus took as He "humbled Himself" (verse 8). Because He humbled Himself, by surrendering to the will of the Father, the Father took action and lifted Jesus up higher and higher. For each step Jesus took downward, the Father delivered an equal, offsetting action that lifted Jesus upward.

Look at that † again. Christ chose to go down, down, down. But God lifted Him up, up, up. This is the transformation process. Our human nature wants to go up, up, up, but that is not in the mind of Christ. When His mind becomes our mind, we see the fruit of first stepping down.

Pharaoh showed that he was deeply infected with the human sin gene for which he continually refused the cure, the surrender to the will of God. God asked him, "How long will you refuse to humble yourself before Me?" (Ex. 10:3). Pharaoh's decision to ignore God's plea destroyed not only him but all of Egypt as well.

"Whoever exalts himself will be humbled, and he who humbles himself will be exalted" (Matt. 23:12). Beware that when we reach the pinnacle of self, falling into temptation, the Father will step in and humble us. It's not an exciting thought.

"The foundation of the plan of salvation was laid in *sacrifice*. Jesus left the royal courts and became poor, that we through His poverty might be made rich. All who share this salvation, purchased for them at such an infinite sacrifice by the Son of God, will follow the example of the True Pattern. . . . Each must have a spirit of self-denial and self-sacrifice."[1]

Without the mind of Christ, we are doomed! We need it to experience true transformation.

"There are some who seem to be always seeking for the heavenly pearl. But they do not make an entire surrender of their wrong habits. They do not die to self that Christ may live in them. Therefore they do not find the precious pearl. They have not overcome unholy ambition and their love for worldly attractions. They do not take up the cross and follow Christ in the path of self-denial and sacrifice. Almost Christians, yet not fully Christians, they seem near the kingdom of heaven, but they cannot enter there. Almost but not wholly saved means to be not almost but wholly lost."[2]

That there are trials in this life, there is no doubt, but as long as we allow God to do His work of purification and refinement through them, it's worth the struggle when compared to the glory that awaits us.

And yes, we were created for eternity. Your time here on earth is but a single grain of sand in an endless universe full of endless beaches. Unfortunately, the trophy of eternal life is now found on a battlefield; we're engaged in combat for it, fighting for every inch of ground. The good news is that we aren't on our own. Jesus already fought the worst of battles on our behalf and is ready to lead us the rest of the way. And His example is a remarkable one.

Immediately after He was baptized in the Jordan River, the Holy Spirit guided Him into the desert, where He spent 40 days in prayer and fasting. It is during this time that we find a major component in living a transformed life: "Prayer is the key in the hand of faith to unlock heaven's storehouse, where are treasured the boundless resources of Omnipotence."[3]

Christ spent entire nights conversing with the Father; time became meaningless to Him as He found ultimate comfort wrapped in the arms of the Eternal One. Jesus' prayer life was the anchor that held Him at the side of God the Father, no matter how powerful the waves of adversity beat against Him. This communion was His source of strength.

Immediately after this 40-day prayer and fasting vigil ended, hunger slammed into the Son of man—and the devil was right there to tempt Him. "Turn these stones to bread," the devil enticed. "If You really are the Son of God, prove it!" Would that be a test for you? Of course not; when was the last time you turned stone into bread?

The temptation the devil craftily set before Jesus was certainly compelling. The devil knew exactly what he was doing, because he had been witness to Christ's forming Adam from nothing but dirt. Making bread from a few rocks surely would not be a big deal for the Creator. (Maybe you have turned bread to stone, but that's another subject!)

But Jesus would not use His power to appease His personal needs or desires. As our example, He depended entirely upon the Father's power to overcome the devil's temptations. You and I can beat every temptation of Satan in the same way.

Jesus stood strong because of His constant prayer life. All the time spent in close communion with the Father afforded Him the opportunity to reach into the bank of heaven and make withdrawals of power. He had also been making Scripture deposits for years, so when the time came, the ammunition was there: "Man shall not live by bread alone, but by every word that proceeds from the mouth of God" (Matt. 4:4). It stopped the devil cold in his tracks! If you likewise make regular deposits of prayer and Bible study in the same bank, you will have the funds to draw on when you need them to thwart any temptation.

It's been said, "Bible study will keep you from sinning, but sinning will keep you from Bible study." And again: "A sinning man will stop praying, but a praying man will stop sinning." Examining the results of the battle between Christ and Satan in the wilderness, it's evident that there is much truth in these statements.

Satan tried two more times to tempt Jesus in the wilderness, but the power of the Father working through Jesus was more than he bargained for—Christ, 3; the devil, 0. James stated it perfectly: "Submit to God. Resist the devil and he will flee from you" (James 4:7). This very same power to resist is *always available for us.*

The next description of the new mind that can be ours is so amazing that I often tear up when I think about it. Let's now look to the Garden of Gethsemane, near the end of Christ's earthly ministry. There we find Jesus walking among the olive trees, away from His disciples, seeking a quiet place to pray. He did not want His followers to be witness to His intense grief and suffering. Ellen White describes the scene in this way:

"In the wilderness of temptation the destiny of the human race had been at stake. Christ was then conqueror. Now the tempter had come for the last fearful struggle. For this he had been preparing during the three years of Christ's ministry. Everything was at stake with him. If he failed here, his hope of mastery was lost; the kingdoms of the world would finally become Christ's; he himself would be overthrown and cast out. But if Christ could be overcome, the earth would become Satan's kingdom, and the human race would be forever in his power. With the issues of the conflict before Him, Christ's soul was filled with dread of separation from God. . . . The sins of men weighed heavily upon Christ, and the sense of God's wrath against sin was crushing out His life. . . . In His agony He clings to the cold ground, as if to prevent Himself from being drawn farther from God. . . . From His pale lips comes the bitter cry, 'O My Father, if it be possible, let this cup pass from Me.' Yet even now He adds, 'Nevertheless not as I will, but as Thou wilt.'"[4]

Jesus was in His early 30s; what man that young would want to die? The devil kept telling Jesus that He would never come out of the grave. As a man, Jesus could not see past the tomb and had no way of knowing that victory was assured. Three times He asked the Father to let the cup pass from Him. He did not want to go through with it; as a man, He was scared.

"The awful moment had come. . . . The fate of humanity trembled in the balance. Christ might even now refuse to drink the cup apportioned to guilty man. It was not yet too late. He might wipe the bloody sweat from His brow, and leave man to perish in his iniquity. He might say, Let the transgressor receive the penalty of his sin, and I will go back to My Father. Will the Son of God drink the bitter cup of humiliation and agony? Will the innocent suffer the consequences of the curse of sin, to save the guilty?"[5]

The portal of the tomb loomed large in Jesus' heart. Would that cold, stone edifice become His eternal prison? If He took the sins of humanity upon Himself, would it cause Him to be separated from the Father forever? He desired to be released, but it did not come. When you beg for an answer to prayer and heaven seems like a gigantic steel plate that bounces your requests back to you, remember that Jesus knows the suffering you're experiencing. The answer He wanted did not come, but He loves us so much that He made the choice: If we could not be with Him forever, *He no longer wanted to be God.* He was willing to take the chance of eternal death so that we might live. What amazing love!

It is this special thing He has done, and will do in His power—short of working against your free-choice will—that guarantees you and I can be transformed into His image and become victors in the conflict against evil.

Christians talk a great deal about the cross of Calvary and, indeed, we should. The ornament that so many display in their homes, cars, or around their necks is the cross. But it was in Gethsemane that the battle between good and evil was fought and won: "The words fall tremblingly from the pale lips of Jesus, 'O My Father, if this cup may not pass away from Me, except I drink it, *Thy will be done*."[6]

"Let this mind be in you which was also in Christ Jesus."

You might wonder, "It's easy to say 'Thy will be done,' but there must be more to it!" Yes, there is, and you play a pivotal role.

---

[1] E. G. White, *Testimonies*, vol. 3, p. 387.

[2] E. G. White, *Christ's Object Lessons*, p. 118.

[3] E. G. White, *Steps to Christ*, p. 94.

[4] Ellen G. White, *A Call to Stand Apart* (Hagerstown, Md.: Review and Herald Pub. Assn., 2002), p. 32.

[5] *Ibid.*, p. 33.

[6] *Ibid.* (Italics supplied.)

Chapter 11

The Heavenly
Construction Crew

Tom Boyle, Jr., had suddenly and unexpectedly found himself in the middle of a life-or-death crisis. "Do you see that?" his wife shouted.

Boyle saw it: the crumpled frame of a bike under a car's bumper and, tangled within, a trapped boy. Boyle started running. For an agonizing eternity, the car screeched on, dragging the mass under it. As it finally slowed to a stop, Boyle could hear the small bicyclist screaming and pounding on the car with his free hand. Without hesitation Boyle bent down, grabbed the bottom of the car's chassis, and lifted with everything he had. Slowly, the car's frame rose a few inches. The bicyclist screamed for Boyle to keep lifting, and he let go only after he heard, "It's off me!" Someone had pulled him free, and Boyle let the car back down.

You've probably heard of similar stories of seemingly impossible feats; there are indeed many things hidden in the depths of the human mind and body we don't yet understand. But as a Christian who was once a so-called self-made man in the business world yet who still fell flat on my face as a sinner, I know it's utterly impossible for humans to avoid sinning on their own, no matter how strong our will might be in other areas of life.

How many New Year's resolutions have you broken in your lifetime? "The unaided human will has no real power to resist and overcome evil. The defenses of the soul are broken down. Man has no barrier against sin."[1] Furthermore:

"In this conflict of righteousness against unrighteousness, we can be successful only by divine aid. Our finite will must be brought into submission to the will of the Infinite; the human will must be blended with the divine. This will bring the Holy Spirit to our aid; and every conquest will tend to the recovery of God's purchased possession, to the restoration of His image in the soul."[2]

The struggle on earth between good and evil is all about the battle for that few inches of gray matter between our ears. Who gets ownership?

Who will be in charge? The winner of that struggle determines our ultimate destiny.

A pastor of a small church had recently baptized a young fellow and decided to check in on his spiritual progress. He saw the boy one day and asked, "Son, how are you doing in your walk with the Lord?"

The boy responded, "I'm OK, Pastor. But it feels like two dogs are fighting inside me."

The pastor inquired, "Well, which one is winning?"

After a long pause, as though the boy was trying to dig up an answer from deep within, he finally replied, "The one I say sic 'em to!"

Yes . . . it's that simple! The winner of our spiritual battle is the one we cheer on and cooperate with.

Speaking to a crowd of self-righteous religious leaders, Jesus said, "You are of your father the devil, and the desires of your father you want to do" (John 8:44). The focus on self is a spiritual defect, and unless we change course by the correct exercise of our will, we will stay under the devil's control. Every morning when we roll out of bed, one question needs an absolute answer: "Do I die to self today and invite Jesus in?" To be a part of the royal family, you must humbly kneel down and allow the King to "possess" you. If that sounds offensive, you might suffer from the Peter problem.

The Bible's many stories of Peter's struggles match our own perfectly. As the disciples left the upper room heading toward Gethsemane, their discussion was centered on the soon departing of Jesus. When Peter heard Jesus speak of His sufferings, he piped up, "Lord, why can I not follow You now? I will lay down my life for Your sake" (John 13:37).

This strong, cocky fisherman had walked with Jesus for more than three years, but he had not been converted. He was desperate to be a self-made man and had not surrendered all of himself to Jesus. Don't believe it? Luke 22:31, 32 says, "The Lord said, Simon, Simon, behold, Satan hath desired to have you, that he may sift you as wheat: But I have prayed for thee, that thy faith fail not: and when thou *art converted*, strengthen thy brethren" (KJV).

There it is. After three years of praying, walking, and eating with the Creator, Peter was still not converted! It's just like me: years spent doing all the churchy things but not converted.

Here's an interesting perspective: "Not until he [Peter] had learned his weakness, could he know the believer's need of dependence on Christ.

Amid the storm of temptation he had come to understand that man can walk safely only as in *utter self-distrust* he relies upon the Savior."[3]

"Utter self-distrust"—that is some phrase, isn't it? The word "utter" means absolute, complete, unreserved, or unqualified. It means 100 percent! The word "self" is all about *me!* "Me" is the one who watches out only for himself/herself. Now let's add the word "distrust," which means doubt. We get "100 percent doubt in me."

You must doubt yourself all the time in regard to spiritual matters. It is the only safe course. We cannot expect our own hearts to guide us safely; we need the mind of Christ.

Notice what the Lord says in Ezekiel: "I will give you a new heart [mind] and put a new spirit within you; I will take the heart of stone out of your flesh and give you a heart of flesh" (Eze. 36:26). The phrase "I will," that is, what God will do, is used twice. The bottom line is that God wants us to understand fully the idea that it's all about what *He will* do in us.

There is but one caveat. Not one change can take place until we choose to allow it. The following addresses the proper use of the human will, and it is eye-opening:

"The will is the governing power in the nature of man, bringing all the other faculties under its sway. The will is not the taste or the inclination, but it is the deciding power, which works in the children of men unto obedience to God, or unto disobedience. . . . The will is . . . the power of decision, or choice."[4]

"When you yield up your will to Christ, your life is hid with Christ in God. It is allied to the power which is above all principalities and powers. You have a strength from God that holds you fast to His strength; and a new life, even the life of faith, is possible to you."[5]

"In receiving Christ as our Captain there must be a complete surrender of the human will to the divine will. The Lord can work out His will through those who have made this surrender, for they give prompt and cheerful obedience to His commands."[6]

Your success in overcoming sin hinges upon the surrender of your will to Jesus. And sustaining your commitment means a reliance on daily prayer and Bible study.

The heavenly work crew, the Holy Spirit, had been knocking at my door for some time, and I had finally allowed Him in. At that time the rebuilding of Jim Ayer began. The Holy Spirit has now been living in my home for some time, and He is a great guest. I like the remodeling job He's been doing. Even my wife thinks that He's doing a fine job!

But this is how I see it: At night, when I go to sleep, the Holy Spirit leaves, locks the door of my heart behind Him, and takes a long walk. He doesn't show up again until I wake up in the morning. The interesting thing is that I need to let Him in the house the next morning, because He doesn't have His own key; He doesn't want one. I've tried to give Him a permanent key, but He always says that it is best for our relationship if I offer to let Him back in every day.

Sure, I'm having a little fun with you, but the basis for my fun is anchored in reality. Paul points to this idea in Ephesians 2:21, 22: "In whom the whole building, being fitted together, grows into a holy temple in the Lord, in whom you also are being built together for a dwelling place of God in the Spirit." The heavenly work crew, led by the Master Craftsman, is always ready to rebuild a life. The only stipulation is that He must have complete and unrestricted access to every room of your home.

As we've seen earlier, not everyone makes this choice. This will leave Jesus saying to self-professed Christians on that final day, "I never knew you; depart from Me, you who practice lawlessness," because His construction crew was never invited into their homes (Matt. 7:23).

The people who argue with God about their sin are like Peter and me before we were converted. I was in church every weekend, but I didn't know the Master Craftsman. For more than three years, Peter walked with the Master, but He never fully let Jesus into his home either.

Judas Iscariot suffered from the same problem as Peter. He never learned to have utter distrust in himself, and so he ended up betraying the Son of God.

Judas always hung around the edges of a commitment to Christ, keeping back much of himself in reserve just in case Jesus' kingdom thing didn't pan out. Thinking about his own future, Judas refused to let the heavenly work crew into his home.

But Jesus desperately wanted to help him open the door of his heart. He worked to lead Judas to a radical surrender of his will. You know the story. It was the final evening, just a little before Jesus was to be betrayed into the hands of the mob. Everyone had gathered in the upper dining room for the Passover dinner. By this time Judas had already promised to betray Jesus into the hands of the priests for 30 pieces of silver—the price of a slave. The seats were all arranged, the table was set, and the disciples took their places.

Only one thing was missing: a servant to wash everyone's feet.

These were not feet you and I would be used to. They hadn't seen a pair of socks in their entire lives. These feet shared the same dirty footpaths with farm animals; these feet needed their customary washing before the meal.

There was a problem: Everyone was already seated. Perhaps they believed they were above washing another man's feet. They saw little good in lowering themselves to a servant's role. But Jesus saw differently; He saw with a heavenly mind. He got up, took the servant's washing bowl, got down on His knees, and gently took the feet of Judas and bathed them. This would be His final attempt to knock on the door of Judas' heart so He could enter and transform him.

Christ was asking Judas if he would "let the mind of this Servant be in him," but if there was at all a warm peace that passed through Judas' heart, he repressed it, fought it back, and the willful choice to turn away was made. How often we have likewise let peace slip away because we were not willing to humble ourselves and let Jesus in; how many disciples have been lost over their refusal to surrender?

Peter, on the other hand, experienced a heart-crushing event just a few hours later when he publicly denied his Lord. However, unlike Judas, Peter was humbled. Rather than turn away after his sin, he clung to Jesus, went through the humiliation, and was transformed. He allowed the Lord to rebuild his heart and mind. Peter would no longer be a servant of sin. "Our old man was crucified with Him, that the body of sin might be done away with, that we should no longer be slaves of sin" (Rom. 6:6). Peter finally got it right.

Billy Graham once said about the disciples on the day of Pentecost, "They turned the world upside down because their hearts had been turned right side up!" Their total surrender made all the difference; it works every time. "Everyone may place his will on the side of the will of God, may choose to obey Him, and by thus linking himself with divine agencies, he may stand where *nothing can force him to do evil*."[7]

Isn't that wonderful news? No matter what you've done against God in the past, no matter how low you have fallen into sin, the Lord is willing to forgive and forget. He is always ready to bring His heavenly work crew to your home and begin the reconstruction. The result is victory over sin in this life. "Now having been set free from sin, and having become slaves of God, you have your fruit to holiness, and the end, everlasting life" (verse 22). This is Christ's plan for you!

We just need to be willing to "put off, concerning your former conduct, the old man which grows corrupt according to the deceitful lusts, and be renewed in the spirit of your mind, and that you put on the new man which was created according to God, in true righteousness and holiness" (Eph. 4:22-24). It was "for this purpose the Son of God was manifested, that He might destroy the works of the devil" (1 John 3:8).

When I was in the Dominican Republic some years ago, I was asked by a pastor to conduct a funeral. He was desperate, and the funeral was the next day, so I agreed to help him out. It was only later that I learned that the man who died had utterly hated Christians!

What in the world was I going to say?

The next day I walked the few blocks up the street to the home of the grieving family. People were everywhere, even in the street, waiting for me to begin the funeral. They ushered me into a tiny room, right behind the open coffin. My back was against the wall, yet I was almost belly to belly with the dead man.

I still had no idea what I could say for a man who hated Christians, but suddenly the Holy Spirit gave me a message on the second coming of Christ. As it turns out, I ended up inviting the funeral attendees to the Bible prophecy meetings I was conducting nearby.

What did the dead man think about my topic at his funeral? Nothing; he was dead! That's how we need to be as Christians to the things of this world! Imagine how few problems there would be and how much better everyone in your church would get along if we all were "dead." It sounds funny, but you get the point. It's what God wants . . .

- "Let everyone who names the name of Christ depart from iniquity" (2 Tim. 2:19).
- "My little children, these things I write to you, so that you may not sin" (1 John 2:1).

In 1987 an interesting study on older married couples indicated, "Science is lending support to the old belief that married couples eventually begin to look alike. . . . Couples who originally bore no particular resemblance to each other when first married had, after 25 years of marriage, come to resemble each other, although the resemblance may be subtle, according to a new research report. . . . Moreover, the more marital happiness a couple reported, the greater their increase in facial resemblance."[8]

This idea carries into our relationship with Christ. The longer you and

I walk with Christ and the more time we spend with Him, the more we begin to resemble Him.

My wife and I have been married long enough that we can complete sentences for each other. Spending time together is how that transformation process works. Likewise, the only way you will ever build a friendship with Jesus is to spend more time with Him than you spend with the things of this world.

- "Do you not know that friendship with the world is enmity with God?" (James 4:4).
- "Whoever has been born of God does not sin, for His seed remains in him; and he cannot sin, because he has been born of God" (1 John 3:9).

There are hundreds more Bible texts that speak to these same truths. Clearly God's plan is for you to "go and sin no more." Of course, the devil loves to have you feeling discouraged when reading these texts. The problem is that we often become so attached to our sins that we choose to believe we have no way out.

The devil's lie makes us feel better about ourselves: "The only way anyone will be an overcomer is after we get to heaven. Only then will Jesus be able to help us stop sinning!" It seems unbelievable to think that people are mesmerized by this line, but most are.

What is your concept of God? Many in the church seem to ascribe greater power to the devil. I would suggest they don't appreciate the real power of the God *who kicked Lucifer out of heaven*. The Gospels are full of clashes between Satan and Christ, and there isn't a single time Jesus lost. We can have that same experience.

I've perhaps not seen the beauty, mercy, and power of God more beautifully addressed than this way: "None are so vile, none have fallen so low, as to be beyond the working of this power. In all who will submit themselves to the Holy Spirit a new principle of life is to be implanted; the lost image of God is to be restored in humanity."[9]

Jesus had a special meeting planned on the far side of the Sea of Galilee. On this particular day He would meet up with a man possessed by many demons—a man who has come to be known as the demoniac.

As Jesus and the disciples came ashore, the demoniac started running toward them, yelling and screaming. He was naked; his limbs were bleeding from self-inflicted wounds. What a sight he must have been—certainly enough to scare away anyone who saw him.

Indeed, nobody needed to tell the disciples to get away. They ran as fast as they could back down the beach toward their boat. When they finally reached a safe distance, gasping for air, they turned around for a look. What they saw amazed them.

The demoniac, quiet and calm, was kneeling at the feet of Jesus.

Mark writes about what the disciples saw once they caught up with Jesus again. "They came to Jesus, and saw the one who had been demon-possessed and had the legion, sitting and clothed and in his right mind" (Mark 5:15). This man had been so far gone that he could not even speak to Christ, but Jesus could read his desire for transformation residing deep in his heart. The demoniac was yearning to be set free from the consequences of his life choices and to be restored. Jesus was ready to give those things to him. It was no problem for God; demons fled at His command.

Again, the disciples found the man "in his right mind." I submit to you that Christ shared His own mind with the man and set Him free. Could this encounter be the one from which Paul got his inspiration for writing, "Let this mind be in you"?

And just where did the demoniac get his clothing? I don't know for sure, but I think Jesus took off His outer garment and wrapped it around the man. It's a beautiful picture of justification and sanctification working together in a person. Jesus clothed the man with His righteousness and gave him a new mind. It doesn't get any better than that!

The two most precious gifts in the universe can be ours for the asking, no matter how degenerate we have become. We merely need to raise our eyes heavenward.

I hope you realize that God is far more powerful than Satan. It's time we start believing it, acting like it, and allowing Him to give us daily victories over our giants. In order for victory to occur, however, you must become aware of one of the devil's greatest lies. He might have been telling it to you for your entire life—and you might even believe it.

---

[1] Ellen G. White, *Evangelism* (Washington, D.C.: Review and Herald Pub. Assn., 1946), p. 601.

[2] Ellen G. White, *Our High Calling* (Washington, D.C.: Review and Herald Pub. Assn., 1961), p. 153.

[3] Ellen G. White, *The Acts of the Apostles* (Mountain View, Calif.: Pacific Press Pub. Assn., 1911), p. 515. (Italics supplied.)

[4] Ellen G. White, *Child Guidance* (Nashville: Southern Pub. Assn., 1954), p. 209.

⁵ Ellen G. White, *My Life Today* (Washington, D.C.: Review and Herald Pub. Assn., 1952), p. 318.

⁶ Ellen G. White, *That I May Know Him* (Washington, D.C.: Review and Herald Pub. Assn., 1964), p. 219.

⁷ E. G. White, *Child Guidance*, p. 209. (Italics supplied.)

⁸ Daniel Goleman, reporting in New York *Times,* Aug. 11, 1987.

⁹ E. G. White, *Christ's Object Lessons*, p. 96.

Chapter 12

Temptation

When I was young, I very much enjoyed fishing with my dad. In fact, we even had a secret fishing hole—and did all we could to keep it a secret. We would never fish there if we saw anyone else in the area.

The area is called Kaiser Peak Meadows, a beautiful setting in northern California consisting of grasslands and a swampy bog. It's surrounded by a ranch on one side, a railroad on another, and the road on yet another side. These landmarks merge to form a triangle of land that might have been a lake at one time. But now, only a tiny stream bubbles up from one corner and then gently meanders through the meadow and eventually under train tracks on the other end.

Our secret spot lay adjacent to the railroad tracks, a 10-foot-wide pool of water marked by a giant-sized willow bush. After making sure no one was watching, we had to carefully scamper off the tracks, negotiate an old cattle fence, and sneak toward the hole. The peat-bog was very thick, but we had to walk ever so softly or else our steps would send ripples across the water and scare the fish away. We practically crawled to the hole so that our shadows would not be seen on the water and alert the fish.

Once we were settled as close as we could get to the water's edge, I would bait my hook with the choicest night crawler I could find and a couple of smaller worms that had a lot of wiggle to them. Now the real skill came into play. The branches of the willow hung low, almost down to the water. Dad had taught me to swing my fishing pole back and forth until the worm and line were rocking like a pendulum. Then I would let it fly, attempting to gently caress the top of the water as far back under the willow as I could get.

The rest was up to the fish—and my patience. I would wait, maybe even feel a little tug, wait some more . . . and then *yank!* All of a sudden, the water would explode with a monster German brown trout. As that beautiful bunch of wiggling worms lay on the creek bottom, that hungry trout just could not handle the temptation. He would toy with the worms a little, then suck them into his mouth just far enough so he could carry them back under the bank. Once he thought it was safe to eat, away from prying eyes, he would suck the worms all the way in.

And that's when I had him—all five pounds.

The subject of temptation is one of the most important in the Bible, but it might also be the most misunderstood.

Satan has been studying the human race for a long time and has perfected the very best bait to tempt us. He dangled the beautiful Bathsheba in front of King David and had him hooked. He placed a pagan Babylonian robe in Achan's pathway, and Achan took the bait. He tempted Eve with the promise of godhood, and he snagged her.

Because of the devil's alarming success rate at fishing for sin, we have been duped into the belief that simply seeing a wiggling worm must be sin. In other words, many Christians believe that temptation itself is a sin. Do you think that's true? Even if you don't believe it, I would venture you probably act as though you do anyway.

Years ago an actor by the name of Flip Wilson, after doing something silly onstage, would often say, "The devil made me do it." He made the line famous and would get huge laughs all the time, but the subject really isn't a joking matter. The devil cannot make you do anything. He can only invite you to join him by using the most alluring worms he can invent.

Temptation, dangling on the hook in front of us, is only an invitation to sin—not a foregone conclusion. It becomes sin only if we choose to bite. The apostle John made the relationship between temptation and sin clear when he wrote, "My little children, these things I write to you, so that you may not sin. And *if* anyone sins, we have an Advocate with the Father, Jesus Christ the righteous" (1 John 2:1). There is a world of difference between "if" and actually doing it.

Satan's sole focus is to destroy every hint of Christ in you, which is why he's in the business of tempting you. But when you're faced with what seems like an overwhelming urge to sin, you have an out—God dwelling in you. Every time temptation shows its loathsome face, I urge you to stand on Christ's shoulders; no giant can overcome you. In fact, they'll all run away. "Therefore submit to God. Resist the devil and he will flee from you" (James 4:7).

This is not just wishful thinking. It's a Bible promise. Just as falling out of a tree results in gravity pulling you down to the ground, resisting the devil will result in him bolting from the scene. What once might have appeared to you as an overwhelming battle against all odds will soon evaporate into an empty battlefield.

Yet even with this wonderful, liberating promise, Stockholm syndrome is still pervasive in the church. Most professed Christians will never believe they can have victory over any and every temptation this side of heaven. For them, everyone is destined to go on sinning until Jesus comes. But I suggest this is a cheap kind of grace and, worse, anyone who believes and lives out this sad philosophy is in danger of losing eternal life.

"But of Him you are in Christ Jesus, who became for us . . . righteousness and sanctification and redemption" (1 Cor. 1:30). Everything we need to gain victory is wrapped up in the life of Christ. When you give all there is of you to Him, you'll start having victory even over sins that have taken up residence deep inside your home. Right now, when the stakes are so high, when we are living in the last days of earth's history, we desperately need to understand that we can, indeed, be overcomers.

The following words offer the perfect description of our journey and how the transformation process is to work in us. Take special note of how building our relationship with Christ is paramount in being an overcomer of temptation:

"It is growth in knowledge of the character of Christ that sanctifies the soul. To discern and appreciate the wonderful work of the atonement transforms him who contemplates the plan of salvation. By beholding Christ he becomes changed into the same image, from glory to glory, as by the Spirit of the Lord. The beholding of Jesus becomes an ennobling, refining process. . . . The perfection of Christ's character is the Christian's inspiration. . . . Christ should never be out of the mind. The angels said concerning Him, 'Thou shalt call his name Jesus: for he shall save his people from their sins' (Matthew 1:21, KJV). . . . Assurance, helpfulness, security, and peace are all in Him. He is the dispeller of all our doubts, the earnest of all our hopes. How precious is the thought that we may indeed become partakers of the divine nature, whereby we may overcome as Christ overcame! . . . He is our refuge in the storm. . . .

"The power of Christ is to be the comfort, the hope, . . . of every one that follows Jesus in his conflict, in his struggles in life. He who truly follows the Lamb of God which taketh away the sin of the world can shout as he advances, 'This is the victory that overcometh the world, even our faith' (1 John 5:4, KJV).

"What kind of faith is it that overcomes the world? It is thɛ makes Christ your own personal Savior—that faith which, your helplessness, your utter inability to save yourself, takeↄ .... helper who is mighty to save, as your only hope. It is faith that will not be discouraged, that hears the voice of Christ saying, 'Be of good cheer, I have overcome the world, and my divine strength is yours.'"[1]

The entire tension of the great battle between good and evil is portrayed in these lines. While we have a sad and "utter inability to save" ourselves, that lack is fulfilled by "the power of Christ to save" us from our sins.

In 1 John 2:16 the apostle identifies three specific areas of danger to every Christian. Every sin has its roots anchored in these three categories of temptation. It's all the bait the devil uses to lure us in. Sin is extremely attractive, especially early on in our spiritual development. Why else would we bite? So raise your antenna and always be on guard for the following:

Lust of the flesh: Food, drugs, and alcohol fit into this category, along with many other consumable items. It is evident in our world that this is a major area of temptation. It was part of the temptation that hooked Eve. Abuse of the natural appetite was also the first temptation the devil tried to hook Jesus with when he said, "Turn these stones to bread."

Lust of the eyes: After Eve fell, she ran to Adam as the devil's tempter. Adam saw what she had done and knew that the penalty for her disobedience was death. He looked upon her beauty and decided he desired the woman more than he desired God, so he took the fruit and ate.

Pride of life: So many things fit into this category—but we'll focus on power, fame, and wealth. None of these things are sins in and of themselves, but power, fame, and wealth are easily abused by those who aren't humble before God, and they can become idols to those who seek after them before they seek after God. Satan tempted Eve with power she was not meant to have, and her pride of life won out over her love for God.

This array of sins seems overwhelming, doesn't it? But take each one on an individual basis and you'll see that for "every class of temptations there is a remedy. We are not left to ourselves to fight the battle against self and our sinful natures in our own finite strength. Jesus is a mighty helper, a never-failing support. . . . None need fail or become discouraged, when such ample provision has been made for us."[2]

Satan tried to rob Jesus of His perfection, but Jesus refused to pick up the temptation or consider it closely. Instead, He looked at the temptation just long enough to see it for what it was—an invitation to sin against His

Father. Then by the power of the Father, He turned away. "In His successful resistance He has left us a bright example, that we should follow in His steps. If we are self-confident or self-righteous we shall be left to fall under the power of temptation; but if we look to Jesus and trust in Him we call to our aid a power that has conquered the foe on the field of battle, and with every temptation He will make a way of escape."[3]

Here is an example of how this works in our world. (Remember, transformation is a *process*.) I like to shop at the grocery store and do it every chance I get. My wife doesn't like going with me because I'm a label reader; food fascinates me! I love to cook, so I can spend an hour investigating every new thing on the shelf.

Eventually, after finishing my rounds up and down every aisle, I make my way to the checkout stand, where, invariably, a long line of people with baskets crammed with beer, wine, soda, and junk food stands in my way. The waiting begins. As I'm sure you know, the counter space near these checkout lines is referred to as the "impulse section." Customers are enticed to grab the items as a last-second impulse.

The only things to really look at while you're standing there are the candy, gum, and magazines. The gum and the candy can hold my attention for only so long, so my attention will sometimes move to the magazines. What usually adorns the covers of such magazines as *People, Us, National Enquirer*, and others?

That's right—beautiful women with very few clothes on. It's impulse shopping.

Now at that moment, I have two choices after seeing those photos. Option one, I like what I see and keep looking, or two, I recognize it's the devil's bait, refuse to keep looking, and pray for strength to honor God and resist feeding the lust of the eyes.

With choice number one, gazing upon the magazine and eventually lusting after the woman on the cover, I would eventually fall from temptation into sin. It's a constant battle for most men in this world, and Jesus let us know that satisfying our lusts only in the mind is akin to actually committing it physically. "But I say to you that whoever looks at a woman to lust for her has already committed adultery with her in his heart" (Matt. 5:28). Entertaining sin in the heart is so easy a snare to fall into because the world can't see us do it; we feel safe from judgment. But God can see it. And worse, it numbs us to the reality of the sin and opens the door to further abuse.

With choice number two, however, I decided to turn away, but I was enabled to do so only by the power of Christ's mind—the new mind I acquired that very morning because I spent time with Him in Bible study and prayer. I chose to die to self, acknowledging to God that His choices for me should also be my choices for myself.

We are told, "It was from the Father that Christ constantly drew the power that enabled Him to keep His life free from spot or stain of sin. It was this power that enabled Him to resist temptation."[4] When temptations come knocking, send Jesus to the door! This power is ours for the asking; pray diligently wherever you go. We are destined to be overcomers if we invite Christ to walk with us everywhere.

---

[1] E. G. White, *That I May Know Him*, p. 166.

[2] Ellen G. White, *Mind, Character, and Personality* (Nashville: Southern Pub. Assn., 1977), vol. 1, p. 32.

[3] Ellen G. White, *Maranatha* (Washington, D.C.: Review and Herald Pub. Assn., 1976), p. 82.

[4] Ellen G. White, in *Review and Herald*, July 4, 1912.

Chapter 13

Overcomers

"Overcome" is a word we seldom hear today in a biblical sense. We might hear a news report about someone who was overcome with carbon monoxide fumes or who was overcome with grief, but you won't hear a report about someone who has overcome in Christ.

The Greek word *nikao* means to be victorious and applies to both military combat and legal battles. The New Testament writers used the word to convey the victory of overcoming an enemy in the temporal realm as well as in the spiritual realm.

We find this prevalent in the book of Revelation, chapters 2 and 3 especially. Even better, the words are those of Jesus Christ, who, we're told, is seeking for those who will take His name and overcome as He overcame. Let's look at how Christ uses the word and the reward He promises to those who do overcome:

Revelation 2:7—"To him who overcomes I will give to eat from the tree of life." If you overcome, you will eat from the tree that Adam and Eve were denied because of their sin. Eating from the tree of life results in eternal life!

Verse 11—"He who overcomes shall not be hurt by the second death." Nor will you ever again experience the pain of separation from God.

Verse 17—"To him who overcomes I will give some of the hidden manna to eat. And I will give him a white stone, and on the stone a new name written." Because you allowed God to remake you into an overcomer, you will receive a special name.

Verse 26—"He who overcomes, and keeps My works until the end, to him I will give power over the nations." You will be given a leadership role in God's government.

Revelation 3:5—"He who overcomes shall be clothed in white garments, and I will not blot out his name from the Book of Life; but I will confess his name before My Father and before His angels." Jesus will exalt you before the universe!

Verse 12—"He who overcomes, I will make him a pillar in the temple of My God, and he shall go out no more." You will be a foundational member in God's temple, where Jesus Christ is the chief cornerstone.

Verse 21—"To him who overcomes I will grant to sit with Me on My throne, as I also overcame and sat down with My Father on His throne." You will be seated as a coregent with Jesus!

Revelation 21:7—"He who overcomes shall inherit all things, and I will be his God and he shall be My son." Finally, as the angels look on, Jesus will grant you all that is His.

I hope you are as excited as I am about these promises. God wants to give you a place in His throne room. He knows that we are gladiators involved in a life-or-death struggle against the forces of sin, and He desires to declare you a victor. But more than that, He has already granted you victory through His Son, who has already beaten the enemy on the battlefield.

Jesus won by turning away from every temptation, which is what we must also do to become overcomers and share in the glory of eternity with Christ. It's worth our best effort!

Here's an interesting lesson from Scripture. After Jesus fed the 5,000, the disciples were upset with Jesus because He didn't allow the masses to crown Him their king that very day. All of their dreams as disciples would have been realized if He would have only played to the crowd's emotional surge. Instead, Jesus told His men to get in the boat and head to the other side of the Sea of Galilee while He disbursed the crowd. Talk about throwing cold water on the party!

As they head down the hillside, I imagine the disciples were upset with themselves for not staying and encouraging the masses to proclaim Jesus as king. They clambered into the boat with complaints spilling from their mouths. But as they set off and made their way across the sea, they were given an opportunity to redirect that anger into something else—utter fear—as a huge storm enveloped their boat and threatened to send it to the bottom of the raging sea.

Of course, we know that Jesus never took His eyes off that precious cargo inside that boat. He watched from the hill and saw them struggling against the waves, which grew so large that the disciples believed their boat would be swamped at any moment.

Their minds were totally focused on survival now, and no longer on their cherished pride-driven ideas and dreams of what they thought Christ should be. It was at this time that Jesus chose to make His entrance. Here is an insightful portrayal of the event by Ellen White as featured in *Signs of the Times*, August 11, 1898:

"At last the disciples saw that their efforts were in vain, that they were unable to help themselves. With feelings of remorse they remembered their impatience with Jesus, and called upon God for pardon. And now the time had come for Jesus to help them. Placing His feet upon the waters, He stepped from one white-capped wave to another, as if walking upon dry land.

"The disciples saw the Savior walking upon the water, and they were afraid. They did not recognize their Master, but saw in this apparition an omen of their destruction. But Jesus quieted their fears. Above the roar of the tempest His voice was heard, 'Be of good cheer: it is I: be not afraid.' Then Peter in his joy cried, 'Lord, if it be thou, bid me come unto thee on the water.' Jesus bade him come, and Peter sprang confidently out of the boat, and, with his eyes fixed upon Jesus, stepped from one white wave to another."

Consider the situation. Jesus was walking from "one white-capped wave to another," meaning the waves were giant—big enough, anyway, to scare fishermen who had spent their entire lives on the water. But Peter then got out of the boat, his eyes fixed on Jesus, and also walked from cap to cap.

However, danger struck again. (The devil is persistent!) Peter took his eyes off Jesus and focused on the monster waves around him. It was not unlike the spies in Israel who took their eyes off God and saw only giants in the land. In an instant he was sinking like a rock. He cried out, "Lord, save me." Continuing with the account:

"His prayer was heard. Jesus' hand was stretched out to grasp the sinking Peter, and His voice was heard saying, 'O thou of little faith; wherefore didst thou doubt?' When Jesus was received with Peter into the boat, 'immediately they were to land'—the place where Christ had appointed to meet them."

I admit it—I had always given Peter a bad time about his failure—until one day I thought, *Forget the storm; would I have gotten out of the boat even in calm conditions?* It's true that Peter received a mild rebuke from the Lord, but it wasn't because he didn't trust Jesus when he got out of the boat.

When he got out, he had faith Jesus could take him the distance. It's only on the way that Peter began to sink.

The Lord says, "Go and sin no more." Are you going to get out of the boat of sin because you believe Him? Or are you going to stay in the boat with the rest of the crowd and never test His mighty power to save you from sin?

I think it's interesting that the Bible doesn't tell us how Peter got back to the boat. Did he swim? Did he walk? What do you think? For me, I believe he walked on the water arm in arm with the Savior. On that day Peter had become a water-overcomer. Yes, it would be some time before he learned that the only way to deal with every storm of life is to walk above it alongside the Savior, but he was learning.

This is where your strength for every temptation originates—in Him. What He wants to do in and through you, to make you an overcomer, is mind-boggling. But in order to walk on water, you need to choose to get out of the boat!

Here's a good question: "Why is it that our youth, and even those of mature years, are so easily led into temptation and sin? It is because the Bible is not studied and meditated upon as it should be. If it were made the daily study, there would be an inward rectitude, a strength of spirit, that would resist the temptations of the enemy."*

The study of God's Word signals to the Holy Spirit that we have opened the door of our hearts and are willing for the heavenly work crew to do their work. It is the abiding presence of the Master Craftsman that gives us victory over temptation and sin. It's time to get out of the boat! Once you do, an entirely new dynamic of the Christian experience will open before you.

---

* E. G. White, *Counsels to Parents, Teachers, and Students*, p. 442.

Chapter 14

The Hound of Heaven

The Greek word *meno* means "to abide" and is used—in some form—more than 40 times in the Gospels and the Epistles. It's probably not a coincidence, then, that it's also one of the most important words in the Bible.

When translated into English, *meno* has some variation in meaning, but most focus upon a sense of staying, dwelling, or remaining in. This offers amazing insight into the heart of God and His desire to become one with us. In Genesis 1:26, God says, "Let Us make man in Our image, according to Our likeness." These words are a clue regarding the oneness of the Godhead—it is *Their* likeness—and I believe the glue of this eternal pattern is love.

"Man was . . . designed to be a counterpart of God. . . . Man is very dear to God, because he was formed in His own image."[1] That's an amazing insight into our destiny—to be God's "counterpart." It means "one that closely resembles another or one that has the same functions and characteristics as another" and "one of two parts that fit and complete each other."

How amazing is that? We were created as "one of two parts that fit and complete each other." Yet Adam's and Eve's sinful choices ripped us away from our divine counterpart. Amazingly, the Godhead's love immediately responded to repair this breach. That's what love does—it is the glue that fights to keep us united. That love was seen in Jesus. "We are not left alone to engage in this conflict. Jesus Christ is the Captain of our salvation."[2]

The Godhead established a stunning plan of sacrifice that would be executed far into the future and enable Jesus to provide present help to His children. "So surely as there never was a time when God was not, so surely there never was a moment when it was not the delight of the eternal mind to manifest His grace to humanity."[3] Because of His future sacrifice on their behalf, Jesus was able to offer Adam and Eve His abiding presence—if they would open the door of their hearts and allow Him entrance.

Drastic change has taken place on the earth. Humans now have "the power to quench the Spirit of God; the power of choosing is left with them. They are allowed freedom of action. They may be obedient through the name and grace of our Redeemer, or they may be disobedient, and realize the consequences."[4] But praise God, the Hound of Heaven pursues us with a hunger we can scarcely comprehend. Francis Thompson, the English poet, captured the relentless pursuit of humans by God in his poem "The Hound of Heaven." Here are just a few lines:

> "I fled Him, down the nights and down the days;
> I fled Him, down the arches of the years;
> I fled Him, down the labyrinthine ways
> Of my own mind; and in the midst of tears
> I hid from him. . . .
> Still with unhurrying chase,
> And unperturbed pace,
> Deliberate speed, majestic instancy,
> Came on the following Feet,
> And a Voice above their beat—
> 'Naught shelters thee, who wilt not shelter Me.'"

Praise God that, despite our constant turning away, He continues to follow after us desiring nothing more than to abide with us for eternity.

This pattern of pursuit is traceable, like a golden thread, throughout the Bible. In Genesis 5:22 and Genesis 6:9 we read that "Enoch walked with God," and, "Noah walked with God." Even when few antediluvians chose to walk with the Sinless One, He still searched the land with desperate measure to find one who would.

The pursuit continues in Exodus 29:46: "They shall know that I am the Lord their God, who brought them up out of the land of Egypt, that I may dwell among them." And the next step the Lord took was to command, "Let them make Me a sanctuary, *that I may dwell among them*" (Ex. 25:8). Even in their sinful state, the Lord sought to abide with them. "In their behalf He constantly manifested the riches of His love and patience."[5]

Then, at last, the biggest step ever was taken to reestablish oneness. "'Behold, the virgin shall be with child, and bear a Son, and they shall call His name Immanuel,' which is translated, '*God with us*'" (Matt. 1:23).

It had been nearly 4,000 years of separation, but humanity and divinity were once again united—and in an unbelievable way. Jesus left His glory behind to enter into the human race. John describes it brilliantly: "The Word became flesh *and dwelt among us*, and we beheld His glory, the glory as of the only begotten of the Father, full of grace and truth" (John 1:14).

Each step of His ancient plan has moved the Godhead closer to us. His goal has always been to draw us back into full communion with Himself, striving to remove the barrier of sin so that one day this process can reach its conclusion.

We must commit to join Him in the process. We must invite Him to come and dwell within us, to abide with us in our hearts. It is the abiding process that will cause our hearts to burn within us and free us from sin. He loved us so much to reach across space and time to live with us forever; do we really want to live sinful lives in response to that kind of love?

---

[1] Ellen G. White, in *Review and Herald*, June 18, 1895.

[2] Ellen G. White *Manuscript Releases* (Silver Spring, Md.: Ellen G. White Estate, 1993), vol. 16, p. 96.

[3] Ellen G. White, *God's Amazing Grace* (Washington, D.C.: Review and Herald Pub. Assn., 1973), p. 120.

[4] Ellen G. White, *Gospel Workers* (Washington, D.C.: Review and Herald Pub. Assn., 1915), p. 174.

[5] E. G. White, *Christ's Object Lessons*, p. 288.

Chapter 15

Abiding in a Forever Relationship

On the surface it sounded like a simple request, "Abide with us." Yet the words were packed with transforming power that would change them forever.

If they had been asked to rate on a scale of 1 to 10 how their day had been going up to that point, the two disciples from Emmaus would have rated it a big fat zero. Their dreams had been crushed. They had heard their Master mocked by scores shouting, "He saved others; Himself He cannot save" (Matt. 27:42). They had watched as their hope hung in bloody agony on a Roman cross. Now every inch of the rock-strewn road home rose up to taunt their sorrow and misery.

Suddenly, a stranger, apparently lingering alongside the roadway, drew near to them and asked why they were so sad. We pick up the story in Luke 24:18, as Cleopas responds, "Are You the only stranger in Jerusalem, and have You not known the things which happened there in these days?" And with quivering lips, they both added, "We were hoping that it was He who was going to redeem Israel" (verse 21).

With both of them overflowing with despair, their eyes were hidden from the very One they desired to see again. Perhaps waiting for the perfect teachable moment, the Stranger allowed the scales of darkness to remain upon their eyes. It gave Him opportunity to first unfold the beauty of the Messiah found all throughout their Sacred Scriptures. His desire was to abide with them and to dispel every shred of darkness that was choking out the Light.

The farther they traveled and the longer they listened, the two disciples noticed less the rocky pathway and, strangely, the less their hearts ached as the Light found His way into their hearts. Now, with the sun disappearing behind the hills as they neared their home, the Stranger indicated that He would continue on His journey alone.

But the two disciples were desperate to hear more! They quickly took the initiative to press Him to stay with them awhile longer. They urged, "Abide with us, for . . . the day is far spent" (verse 29). They were just so relentless, He desired to break bread with them before going on.

Taking His place at the table, the Stranger blessed the food in a way that Jesus had always done it. Some have suggested that in the moment He raised His hands with the bread, the nail prints came into view and the disciples recognized Jesus.[1] I can just about hear their explosion of joy—and then *poof*, He vanished from their sight.

In giddy excitement they agreed, "Did not our heart burn within us while He talked with us on the road, and while He opened the Scriptures to us?" (verse 32). Although darkness would shroud their dangerous pathway, the two men burst out the door and dashed into the cool night air, running as fast as their feet could carry them, back over the same road that had caught their tears of agony just hours before. They knew they must return to Jerusalem to tell everyone, "Our Lord is risen!" Darkness was replaced by the Light.

What made the difference? For one thing, they confessed to one another that the burning in their hearts was something they had felt even before they knew the stranger was Jesus. In essence, the change from despair to hope came to them as they experienced the presence of the One who is "altogether lovely" through their traveling Bible study. And this is the key to the indwelling presence of Jesus in your life:

"It would be well for us to spend a thoughtful hour each day in contemplation of the life of Christ. We should take it point by point, and let the imagination grasp each scene, especially the closing ones. As we thus dwell upon His great sacrifice for us, our confidence in Him will be more constant, our love will be quickened, and we shall be more deeply imbued with His spirit."[2]

Do you want to experience a greater measure of the Holy Spirit in your life? The study of God's Word is fundamental to that end!

When you open the Bible, Jesus will walk alongside you, just as He walked with the disciples to Emmaus, with Adam and Eve in the cool of the garden, and as He did with Enoch and Noah. He will guide your every step, dispelling darkness with the light of truth.

Another fundamental step: If the two disciples had not pressed the invitation upon Christ to abide with them, He would have continued on His journey. The Savior would have walked out of their lives, and their loss might have been eternal.

How can I make that statement? Many Bible texts offer a strong indication that this was the case. In Mark 6:48, for instance, the disciples were caught at sea in a horrific storm and near the point of exhaustion when Jesus approached: "About the fourth watch of the night He came to them, walking on the sea, and would have passed them by." Without crying out to Jesus, they would have been lost at sea.

The clincher, however, is found in Revelation 3:20: "Behold, I stand at the door and knock. If anyone hears My voice and opens the door, I will come in to him and will dine with him." Jesus only knocks on the door; He does not break it down! After some period of time passes, if no one answers, Jesus will eventually—however sadly—depart.

How long does He continue to knock? Only He knows that answer. It is left with you and me to extend the invitation to Jesus to abide with us, because He will never force Himself upon us or take away our freedom to choose. Love and freedom are the basis of His kingdom.

Make no mistake: God *wants* you to answer the door and invite Him in. He leaves not because He wants to, but because you want Him to. A good friend, Herbert Douglass, once told me, "Abiding is merely an English word describing this innate attitude called agape. God can't be anything other than who He is." God is love, and He wants to share that love with you.

The devil attempted to destroy the beautiful plan of God to abide with His children, but the Creator persisted, "Let them make Me a sanctuary, that I may dwell among them" (Ex. 25:8). He wasn't going to allow anything to separate Him from what He loves! "Christ was their instructor. . . . In the tabernacle and the temple His glory dwelt in the holy shekinah above the mercy seat."[3]

Do you realize just how special you are? The rebellion that began in heaven did not rear its ugly head anywhere else in the vast creation of God—only here on our planet. It is here that the Godhead chose to focus all of His redemptive power and abiding energy. "The Word became flesh and dwelt among us, and we beheld His glory" (John 1:14).

Can you fathom such amazing love directed at you? This is the reason God's love will be a wonder for all eternity. We will never be able to probe fully the depths of His desire to abide with us. "I will pray the Father, and He will give you another Helper, that He may abide with you forever" (John 14:16).

This is the promise we're given: "Abiding in Christ, we become one with Him. Then we are safe, entirely safe, against all the assaults of Satan."[4] As God dwells within us, we will be safe from every temptation the devil sets before us—but remember that God does not beat down the door. He might pound aggressively to get our attention, but we must open it! "Every warning, reproof, and entreaty in the word of God or through His messengers is a knock at the door of the heart. It is the voice of Jesus asking for entrance."[5] If, however, you continue to ignore the knocking, at some point you might no longer hear the sound of it.

I grew up in a small northern California town that had just 3,500 residents. The only thing that broke the quietude of the sleepy mountain community was the Southern Pacific Railroad train on its journey through the valley.

One day that all changed with a piercing racket. Startled, everyone in town immediately focused on the noise; it was the sound of bells that were newly installed in the tower of the Catholic church. It clanged every half hour all day long. So much for the sleepy little town!

Still, some months passed, and by then I noticed that I didn't notice the bells. I wondered, *What happened to those terrible bells?* But in fact, they were still there, clanging every half hour, just as before. The difference was that my brain had adjusted to the sound, and I had become totally oblivious to it. "With every knock unheeded, the disposition to open becomes weaker. The impressions of the Holy Spirit if disregarded today will not be as strong tomorrow. The heart becomes less impressible, and lapses into a perilous unconsciousness of the shortness of life, and of the great eternity beyond."[6]

Your sins tear at the heart of God, but the thought of not spending eternity with you was so much more than He could endure that it drove Him to agonize in Gethsemane and to pour out His blood at the cross. He gave Himself as a love offering so you could enjoy a forever relationship with Him. "Behold, the tabernacle of God is with men, and He will dwell with them, and they shall be His people. God Himself will be with them" (Rev. 21:3).

God's desires for you are quite simple:
1. That you would humble yourself, allowing the old to die to make room for the new.
2. That you would have the victorious mind of Christ become yours.
3. That you would allow Him to establish residence in His earthly temple—you.

4. That you would allow His brightness to destroy every sin found in your life.
5. That you would allow Him to dwell in you to establish an impenetrable barrier against every temptation of the devil.
6. That you would allow Him to lift you up, higher and higher.

Your choice to become a part of God's plan will complete the circle. After 6,000 years of sorrow, the Godhead's longing desire for our restoration to full fellowship will be satisfied. "At that day you will know that I am in My Father, and you in Me, and I in you" (John 14:20). It seems that we are to be spiritually interwoven with God; harmony will be restored!

"But unless the members of God's church today have a living connection with the Source of all spiritual growth, they will not be ready for the time of reaping."[7] That is why God is inviting you now to participate in this living connection, whereby you will continually receive spiritual nourishment from the Source of all life: "I am the vine, you are the branches. He who abides in Me, and I in him, bears much fruit; for without Me you can do nothing" (John 15:5).

It really is simple: We can do all things through Christ. All things would certainly include always rejecting temptation and overcoming sin.

However, as the father of lies, the devil continually attempts to blind us. He says we have no choice but to fail, and it's a strong delusion that has fooled the majority of the church. He believes, "Everyone will fail when faced with my temptations." Make no mistake; his delusions are strong. But we can do all things with Jesus abiding in us.

So if you are still having doubts as to what God can fully accomplish in and through you, you're going to love the next chapter.

---

[1] E. G. White, *The Desire of Ages*, p. 800.
[2] *Ibid.*, p. 83.
[3] E. G. White, *Christ's Object Lessons*, p. 288.
[4] Ellen G. White, in *Signs of the Times*, Oct. 10, 1892.
[5] E. G. White, *The Desire of Ages*, pp. 489, 490.
[6] *Ibid.*, p. 490.
[7] E. G. White, *The Acts of the Apostles*, p. 55.

Chapter 16

A Mighty Witch

I met Ragasa while filming in Madagascar. She had large eyes that radiated love, but that was not always the case. As a little girl, she grew up with demons in her home. They not only were seen by all of her family, but also carried on regular conversations with them as well.

When she was a little older, the demons said to her, "We would like you to become a witch. If you agree, we will give you great power." She agreed.

They then instructed her, "Go down to the river. We will meet you there." As commanded, Ragasa made her way to the water's edge. There the demons told her to go "down into the water." She did as they said, and, according to her, she spent the next day and a half under water.

At this moment, I stopped the interview because I thought the interpreter had made a mistake. I asked her to repeat what she had said. And as it turned out, I heard it right—she had lived under water for more than a day. "While there," she explained, "the demons fed me and took care of me." This was all under water! But it doesn't end there. "They then gave me great powers, such as control over lightning. I could be shot with a gun and not be hurt. One day an army came to take over my village, but I created potions that kept them away."

The devil has great power. I have seen many more instances of his fearsome influence demonstrated around the world. And indeed, he is the most powerful created being in the entire universe. "You were the anointed cherub who covers; . . . you were on the holy mountain of God; you walked back and forth in the midst of fiery stones" (Eze. 28:14).

If you think you can contest against this much power, you are greatly mistaken. The Gospels are replete with stories of Satan's power. I'm not telling you these things to panic you; it's just the nature of this war. The apostle Paul wrote that we are not fighting "against flesh and blood, but against principalities, against powers, against the rulers of the darkness of this age, against spiritual hosts of wickedness in the heavenly places" (Eph. 6:12).

But we have a mighty Champion who will fight for us. And when He lives in you, the devil cannot defeat you. In fact, it's an absolute impossibility for the devil to cause you to stumble when God is in charge of your life and holding you up! Ragasa's testimony bears witness to this truth:

"One day the demons were mad at me, and they made me very sick. I went to doctors, but they could do nothing for me. I spent much time in bed." She had learned what most of us know all too well: The devil is sly. At first sin fascinates; then it assassinates.

"A little later two young women came to me and said, 'There is a God in heaven who can heal you. Can we pray for you?'" I thought, *Well, the devil hasn't been doing anything for me lately, so go ahead.* So they prayed for me, and I was immediately healed. Then they told me to learn about Jesus, that it would be a blessing to me. I did as they said, and I fell in love with Jesus and was soon baptized in the river next to my home."

But even at her baptism, the devil was desperate to steal her away from God. "As I came up out of the water, the devil burned my house to the ground. I poked through the ashes after they cooled, looking for my Bible. When I found it, I saw that it hadn't been touched by the fire or the smoke. Because of that miracle, many people in my village believed in God."

Hearing her testimony reminded me of the ancient story when God revealed to King Nebuchadnezzar that his kingdom would not go on forever. The king did not like the prediction, so he decided to build a 90-foot image of himself in gold on the plain of Dura. He then commanded everyone to worship the image as a show of loyalty to his authority.

When three young Hebrews—Shadrach, Meshach, and Abednego—chose to follow God rather than bow to that idol, they were dragged before the king. Furious at their rebellion, Nebuchadnezzar commanded that they be burned to death. The furnace of execution was heated to such an intensity that it actually killed the soldiers who cast in the three men.

But the result was not what had been expected. The astonished king inquired, "'Did we not cast three men bound into the midst of the fire?' They answered, . . . 'True, O king.' 'Look!' he answered, 'I see four men loose, walking in the midst of the fire; and they are not hurt, and the form of the fourth is like the Son of God'" (Dan. 3:24, 25).

The three Hebrews then stepped out of the flames as the king and his counselors gathered around. They were stunned as they looked upon those on "whose bodies the fire had no power; the hair of their head was not singed nor were their garments affected, and the smell of fire was not on them" (verse 27).

Do you love these stories of God's protection? Well, He is the same yesterday, today, and forever. He once frustrated the plans of the devil in ancient Babylon, and He has frustrated the devil's plans in Madagascar. He'll do the same for you.

With the story of her home's destruction fresh on her lips, Ragasa looked at me with a huge grin and said, "I need to build a church. I have 100 people who now believe in Jesus Christ—all of those with whom I've shared my faith."

God is, and will always be, more powerful than the devil! He can always change what seems like sure defeat into certain victory. He is asking you to choose the winning side! He is fully capable of transforming you into His image, into His likeness, regardless of how your present circumstances appear. All He needs is your cooperation and a willing heart.

Andrew Murray, the famous pastor from South Africa, once said, "O my Father, reveal within me what it means, lest I sin against Thee by saying it and not living it." We must have this same introspective spirit. According to Samuel Chadwick, "the Pentecostal gift of the Spirit is the gift of a God-possessed personality. . . . It turns ordinary persons into extraordinary personalities." Ragasa discovered the transforming power of God and made the choice to allow Him to change her. You have the same choice. Say yes to God!

We are destined to become royalty in the courts above, but we must have the authority and power to prepare us for it here and now. "A character formed according to the divine likeness is the only treasure that we can take from this world to the next."* Why not prepare for heaven by asking God to transform you into an overcomer today?

Just prior to His departure from earth, Jesus told His followers to remain in Jerusalem until they received the promise of the Father. What was that promise? "You shall receive power when the Holy Spirit has come upon you; and you shall be witnesses to Me" (Acts 1:8). We can do nothing without the fire of His presence burning within us; we need His fire within. And that fire within gives us the power to be an extraordinary witness for Him—in word and action.

---

* E. G. White, *Christ's Object Lessons*, p. 332.

Chapter 17

The Fire Within

A French explorer journeyed deep into the Congo while on safari many years ago. Each night his guides would gather up sticks, branches, and dry blades of grass as tender for building a large fire to illuminate and protect the camp. They would stoke the fire all night long to keep wild animals from venturing too close.

As their jungle travels continued across many miles, the Frenchman began to notice large piles of sticks and dry grass arranged in exactly the same way as his guides had done each night to prepare their fires. "Who is doing this?" he asked one of the guides.

"The monkeys," came the reply. "They watch us every day and mimic our actions. They have everything right except the fire."

If God removed the Holy Spirit from your church or your life, would anyone be able to tell the difference?

Regarding most Christians today, you'll find a startling contrast between Jesus' promise of power at Pentecost and their present condition. Where is the fire? Many lives have become nicely stacked piles of wood that look good but provide neither light, heat, nor protection. We need the fire of God in our churches and in our lives! The Holy Spirit is essential to the life of the church and the formation of our characters.

We can also go one step further:

"The traits of character you cherish in life will not be changed by death or by the resurrection. You will come up from the grave with the same disposition you manifested in your home and in society. Jesus does not change the character at His coming. *The work of transformation must be done now.* Our daily lives are determining our destiny."[1]

The indwelling Sprit will lead to massive changes in your life. It will . . .
    (1) bring the mind of Christ to the pleading soul
    (2) provide deliverance from sin

(3) awaken dry bones to new life

(4) energize through the power of God

(5) lead and guide: "This is the way"

(6) teach and provide efficiency in service

(7) bring effectiveness to witnessing.

How can we ever do without the fire?

H.M.S. Richards, Sr., a powerful theologian, once lamented, "Some churches are so cold you could skate down the center aisle." And when the fire of the Spirit dies out, superficial ritualism replaces Him.

"Any church that is man-managed instead of God-governed is doomed to failure. A ministry that is college trained but not Spirit-filled works no miracles. The church that multiplies committees and neglects prayer may be fussy, noisy, enterprising, but it labors in vain and spends its strength for naught. It is possible to excel in mechanics but fail in dynamic. There is a superabundance of machinery; what is needed is power. To run an organization needs no God. Man can supply the energy, enterprise, and enthusiasm for things human. The real work of the church depends on the power of the Spirit."[2]

Jesus spoke of this need: "Without Me you can do nothing" (John 15:5). "Nothing" is rather all-inclusive, wouldn't you say? Jesus says we can't do a single thing for ourselves, our churches, or the world in the great cosmic war. We can't defend ourselves without Him. We cannot hope to make it to heaven without the aid of the Spirit dwelling within us, heating us up with His fire. We need to do more than just "play" church with sticks.

Although I was a church member and looked the part, I had no idea what I was missing by not being fully engaged and committed to God's plan for my life. There was an entire spiritual world operating around me of which I was completely unaware. So unless "we are daily advancing in the exemplification of the active Christian virtues, we shall not recognize the manifestations of the Holy Spirit in the latter rain. It may be falling on hearts all around us, but we shall not discern or receive it."[3] This described me perfectly.

It was only after I truly surrendered my life to Him that my spiritual eyes were opened and I saw that God was doing something amazing. So what are spiritual eyes?

A Syrian king went to make war against Israel, but every battle plan he fashioned seemed to be leaked to the enemy. Every effort to entrap and destroy them was frustrated. Finally the king called in his top brass and asked them who the traitor could be. A member of the court spoke up and fingered Israel's prophet, Elisha, who somehow saw their war plans fashioned in secret. The prophet could be found in Dothan.

Enraged, the king sent a vast army to surround the city. The prophet would surely not escape the king's vengeance! Early the next morning Elisha's servant woke up, saw the army, and then ran in a fright to his master.

Elisha attempted to calm his servant: "Do not fear, for those who are with us are more than those who are with them" (2 Kings 6:16). It didn't make sense; the servant's eyes were telling him that they were in big trouble. How could they survive such a huge army?

Then Elisha prayed to God on behalf of his quaking servant: " 'Open his eyes that he may see.' Then the Lord opened the eyes of the young man, and he saw. And behold, the mountain was full of horses and chariots of fire all around" (verse 17). When your spiritual eyes are opened, you can see God's mighty spiritual workings in the physical world. And what a sight to see! Elisha's servant saw an army of fire![4]

Once his eyes had been opened, he beheld God's activity on their behalf—angels sent to give them victory! In Psalm 34:6-8 King David shares, "This poor man cried out, and the Lord heard him, and saved him out of all his troubles. The angel of the Lord encamps all around those who fear Him, and delivers them. Oh, taste and see that the Lord is good; blessed is the man who trusts in Him!"

Today our culture turns to comic book heroes for comfort at a time we should be turning to God. King David observed, "By the word of the Lord the heavens were made, and all the host of them by the breath of His mouth" (Ps. 33:6). Our God is the real deal. His power is awesome, and His love for you is everlasting. His armies are ready and willing to help you overcome the armies of Satan—even before you call upon Him. "Before they call, I will answer; and while they are still speaking, I will hear" (Isa. 65:24).

When I finally did answer Christ's call to recommit my life to Him, He opened my eyes to the spiritual realm. I was amazed at what I saw. The Holy Spirit was and is now being poured out around the world, and I had not recognized it even while sitting in my church. I was one of the "frozen chosen." If that's your present temperature, ask God to give you His fire.

He is giving fire to seekers around the world. Here are some marvelous examples:

The Masai Fortuneteller

Leaving the orphanage, we said our goodbyes to the smiling Masai children, many of whom had simply been left there by family. It was difficult to comprehend that those lovable little ones were intentionally left behind. Unfortunately, cattle are far more precious than children to the Masai. If a child hinders their trek to reach water for the animals, they will leave the child behind. Nothing is more sacred than their cattle.

Rambling southward along the dusty roads of Kenya in our 4 x 4, we crossed the border into Tanzania on our way to a Masai village deep in the bush. We had traveled for much of the morning, enjoying the occasional giraffe poking its head above the trees and watching the hyenas hunkered down in the cool mud ponds near the roadway.

Finally, after we had twisted in and around tiny roads and trails, we popped out into a small clearing. About 100 people appeared to be meeting under a large stick structure and, as it turned out, we learned they had been waiting for us.

I was soon introduced to an older Masai. He had a gleam in his eye, a bright flower-covered blanket wrapped around him, and a very interesting story to share. We sat together at the base of a large termite mound, and he began to speak in Kiswahili—good thing my interpreter was near. He said, "I was the village fortuneteller. I was very wealthy with many cattle."

"How many did you have?" I asked.

He drew back into a relaxed position and said, "Oh, maybe 400." That many cattle meant that he was probably once the most powerful man in the village, if not the entire region!

He soon confided to me that he had regularly "talked to the spirits and demons to gain information. I would not tell someone who came to me what they should do until I negotiated my price. If they didn't pay me, I didn't tell them!" A momentary smile decorated his lips, but he soon became very serious. "One day two men showed up at my village and told me that what I was doing was of the devil and that I needed to stop. I told them to go away. But when I turned on my radio to listen to the BBC news, I came across a broadcast by Adventist World Radio [AWR]. I heard people talking about the Jesus that these men had talked about. I decided to listen. Soon I accepted Jesus into my life."

His wife was sitting next to him, so I asked, "What about your wife? Did she accept Him also?" She grinned practically from ear to ear as he confirmed that she had. I then asked what changes he had made since accepting Jesus.

"I no longer speak to the demons. I no longer tell people their fortune or use the tools of my former trade." The couple even gave up their jewelry.

I had to know more! "What do you do now?"

Pointing in the direction of the large gathering, he said, "I am the leader of that church." I could tell he had the fire! Life with his Lord had become his most sacred possession.

Shiva to Solomon

Benjamin Schoun, the president of AWR at the time, and I were in eastern Nepal, where we secretly participated in several baptisms. It was illegal to promote Christianity then, so we sought the refuge of a mountain stream. After a wonderful day of celebration in the cold waters of the Himalayas, we met a young man building a bamboo home.

His name was Shiva, after the Hindu destroyer god that many people in Nepal and India worship. Somehow Shiva had heard about Jesus and decided to follow Him, but everyone in his village gave him so much trouble that he turned back to the millions of false Hindu gods.

However, by divine appointment, he once again heard about Jesus— this time through AWR's broadcasts. His resolve became stronger as the Spirit drew him in; he felt he must follow the true God this time, no matter the personal cost.

With the radio program as his constant companion, he grew in strength, and it mattered not what friends, neighbors, or even family had to say against his faith. The fire of the Spirit emboldened him to speak for Christ, and he did so eloquently, in fact, that many family members accepted Jesus! And not long after that, he had so many more new believers coming to his home that he decided to erect a large bamboo cross. Imagine that! A village of persecution had become a haven for Christians. Oh, yeah—Shiva also changed his name to Solomon.

Blinded by Angels

In a country whose name I cannot disclose for security reasons, AWR was quietly arranging for new converts to leave the nation in order to train them as church leaders.

They had once been animists living in a country that was not friendly toward Christians, to say the least. The only gospel information they received came to them via AWR shortwave radio programs, which produced awesome results! As nearly as we can tell now, tens of thousands serve Jesus Christ in these remote areas today.

On one particular day about 10 men of faith were sneaking down a jungle pathway, almost ready to cross a river, when all of a sudden police stormed up the bank, their guns and bayonets glaring in the sun. The police yelled and pointed, "There they are; get 'em!"

There was no place for the Christians to run. They froze in silence, waiting to be arrested or killed on the spot for their faith. The police rushed toward them, but suddenly they stopped about 10 feet from the frightened believers. There they stood transfixed; the officers looked confused. One spoke: "Where did they go?" Confusion reigned among the heavily armed men.

Brief seconds passed that felt like an eternity to the brethren. Then a frantic yell: "There they go!" One officer pointed while motioning to the others, and then they were gone as quickly as they had appeared.

Awe and gratitude overwhelmed the Christians. Those who had been a clear and present danger to them were now running after shadows, leaving the team to travel onward to their Bible-training sessions in safety and unharmed.

The Boxing Champ

I met Mahail in the Ukraine several years ago. He looked exactly as I had always imagined a champion boxer from the old Soviet Union would look like—big body and hands, a square jaw—a powerful man. He was also a man who was once fully committed to the Communist cause.

On this day, however, he was thrilled to be showing me his graduation certificate from an AWR Bible correspondence school in Tula, Russia. The area was once the heart of weapons production for the Soviet war machine; however, today 1,500 government radio stations that once barked the party line now share the message of a soon-coming Savior!

Back before the fall of the Soviet Union, after having proudly showed himself to be a strong fighter in the ring, Mahail was offered the opportunity to attend medical school. He was grateful for the chance to serve his country in that capacity. A few short weeks before graduation, a classmate voiced a question to one of the instructors: "Could there be the possibility of a God?" The reaction was swift; the curious student was removed from medical school and not allowed to graduate. Mahail had the same question lingering in his heart, but now he dared not voice it to anyone.

Still, for decades he worked in the medical field and was about ready to retire; his desire for service had evaporated. But then, while trying to find a news station on the radio, Mahail heard the AWR broadcast and new life and joy filled his soul. God lit a match, and soon Mahail's heart was ablaze with the fire of the Spirit.

Mahail soon contacted the AWR studio in Tula and began to receive Bible studies. His question about the existence of God was profoundly answered. He shared with me that he then made the decision to continue in the medical field to help tuberculosis patients. He smiled as he explained, "My practice has taken on a new life. I now pray with all of my patients and point them to the Creator."

Have you recognized the activity of the Holy Spirit working in and around you lately? If the Spirit has taken up residence in your life, you won't need to pause before answering that question. You'd give a resounding yes!

This Spirit is what took hold of Peter once he died to self and rose in Christ. "When the Day of Pentecost had fully come, they were all with one accord. . . . There appeared to them divided tongues, as of fire, and one sat upon each of them. And they were all filled with the Holy Spirit" (Acts 2:1-4).

The result was profound. "By the cooperation of the divine Spirit, the apostles did a work that shook the world. To every nation was the gospel carried in a single generation. . . . Not in their own power . . . but in the power of the living God."[5]

In this spirit, Ellen White makes a profound statement and poses a tough question for each of us to answer: "For the daily baptism of the Spirit every worker should offer his petition to God."[6] "Since this is the means by which we are to receive power, why do we not hunger and thirst for the gift of the Spirit? Why do we not talk of it, pray for it, and preach concerning it?"[7]

The fire of the Spirit is the crowning gift of love given by God to us. Should we not desire it above all things in this world? The ultimate price was paid to deliver this gift—"Do you not know that your body is the temple of the Holy Spirit who is in you, whom you have from God, and you are not your own?" (1 Cor. 6:19). It is only through this power that God can transform us into citizens fit to dwell in His eternal kingdom.

Do you thirst for the righteousness of Christ? If not, you need to do some introspection about your faith, because it will soon be too late! On every hand, the signs of Christ's coming are being fulfilled. Here's a startling observation regarding the situation existing in the church just prior to the return of Christ: "As the storm approaches, a large class who have professed faith in the third angel's message, but have not been sanctified through obedience to the truth, abandon their position and join the ranks of the opposition."[8] This is the only solution:

"The Holy Spirit seeks to abide in each soul. If it is welcomed as an honored guest, those who receive it will be made complete in Christ. The good work begun will be finished; the holy thoughts, heavenly affections, and Christlike actions will take the place of impure thoughts, perverse sentiments, and rebellious acts."[9]

For much of my life, as a practitioner in the fighting arts I've enjoyed martial-arts movies. (I am getting the victory over it!) In every one of these movies, as the action builds, the star is invariably surrounded by dozens of sword-wielding scoundrels ready to attack and kill. The hero takes on all of them at once and often doesn't receive even a trophy scratch. And it never fails: he always emerges victorious. I would always turn to my wife and say, "How corny is that? That could never happen in real life."

But let me share some amazing battles that were, in fact, very real. "Shamgar . . . killed six hundred men of the Philistines with an ox goad; and he also delivered Israel" (Judges 3:31). Were you tempted to think, *It could never happen in real life?* Wait! There are even more stories that will blow you away.

Near the end of King David's life, he recounted the exploits of some of his great men who served him for many years. One of those men at the top of his list was Adino the Eznite, who killed 800 at one time. Another of David's mighty men was Abishai, who used a spear to dispatch 300 enemies in one battle (see 2 Sam. 23:8, 18).

Let's look at one more mighty warrior—Samson. A thousand men surrounded a single warrior armed with only a jawbone of a donkey—not a typical weapon! The result? "With the jawbone . . . I have slain a thousand men" (Judges 15:16). Think about it! If Samson killed one man every 15 seconds, it would have taken him more than four hours of nonstop combat to get the job done. "Unbelievable," you say? Sure—if you don't take into account one very important ingredient: God.

The Bible records, "The Spirit of the Lord came mightily upon" Samson just before he engaged the Philistines in battle (verse 14). And twice in the same chapter of 2 Samuel, David explains that it was the Lord who worked "a great victory" through his mighty men (2 Sam. 23:10). What can we take from this? There is no limit to what one person can do when he or she is filled with the fire of the Spirit.

Now, on the flip side, we find a very sad admission regarding one of Israel's tribes during an ancient battle to fight God's enemies: "The children of Ephraim, being armed and carrying bows, turned back in the day of battle" (Ps. 78:9). They not only turned their backs that day, but apparently it became part of their DNA. In Revelation 7 John names the tribes that stand as representatives of those who will be found in heaven as overcomers. The tribe of Ephraim did not make the list!

It is not about the weapons or the number of those standing against you; it is not about the number of temptations; it is about a God-possessed personality. God can do more with, in, and through one person committed to Him than He can do with an entire army not fully committed to serve Him. You can slay a thousand sins with a single Bible promise.

Will you commit to being that Spirit-filled, God-possessed personality? If you do, you will discover that there will no longer be any more "invincible" giants in your life.

---

[1] E. G. White, *The Adventist Home* (Nashville: Southern Pub. Assn., 1952), p. 16. (Italics supplied.)

[2] Samuel Chadwick, *The Way to Pentecost* (Christian Literature Crusade, February 2001).

[3] Ellen G. White, in *Review and Herald*, Mar. 2, 1897.

[4] During another time and place God sent an angel to do battle with Sennacherib, king of Assyria. "The angel of the Lord went out, and killed in the camp of the Assyrians one hundred and eighty-five thousand; and when people arose early in the morning, there were the corpses—all dead" (2 Kings 19:35). That was just one angel sent by God to protect His children, yet "ten thousand times ten thousand, and thousands of thousands" await His every command (Rev. 5:11).

[5] E. G. White, *Evangelism*, p. 706.

[6] E. G. White, *The Acts of the Apostles*, p. 50.

[7] *Ibid.*

[8] E. G. White, *The Great Controversy*, p. 608.

[9] Ellen G. White, *Counsels on Health* (Mountain View, Calif.: Pacific Press Pub. Assn., 1923), p. 561.

Chapter 18

No Giants in Jericho

Remember Rahab, the pagan prostitute who became an ancestor of Jesus?[1] As you will recall, her amazing transformation in Jericho took place because she was determined to follow the one true God. She did all she could to get closer to Him and His people.

Not long after that event, Joshua was nearing Jericho, a city situated in the land of the giants—the really big guys who caused an entire generation to lose out on the Promised Land. Yet the giants were no longer in the land. Why? Because God finally found devoted followers who believed His promises and acted accordingly. Caleb was such a person, one of two faithful spies from the very beginning. He stood before Israel and pleaded with the people to go forward and take the land, but instead, weeping and faithless, they turned back to the desert.

Some 45 years later, at 85 years old, Caleb was still going strong physically—and so was his faith. The first thing he did after helping to conquer Jericho was to say to Joshua, "Give me this mountain of which the Lord spoke in that day; for you heard in that day how the Anakim were there, and that the cities were great and fortified. It may be that the Lord will be with me, and I shall be able to drive them out as the Lord said" (Joshua 14:12).

Now, many of the Anakims were giants, and they controlled the territory Caleb sought to possess. He wanted to prove that God was well able to make good on His promise spoken some 40 years before. And indeed, men and women who are ablaze with the Holy Spirit are invincible.

Hence, Jericho is a good destination for us to revisit as we sum up.

While I can't possibly know all of the giants of temptation that stand before you, I have some idea. I face many of them myself, and I receive prayer requests from the world over into my office that say we aren't alone. The list of temptations that the devil sets before us is as long as the earth is old. The following letter is both sad and graphic, but I share it with you for a purpose:

"Please pray for me. I am a *victim* of adultery, fornication, homosexuality, and masturbation. I have tried to stop these but am unable. I am a *victim* of these for more than 20 years. I was baptized 11 years ago. Please help me, and pray for me to stop this sinful living."[2]

This poor person was battling real giants, just as you and I do. I absolutely concede that they are not a figment of our imaginations, but what they *are not* are indestructible and undefeatable! We don't need to be *victims*. We become victims only through our own choices.

Perhaps you think I'm being too harsh? Well, consider this: The apostle Paul addressed the very sins our letter writer admits enslave him. He writes, "Walk in the Spirit, and you shall not fulfill the lust of the flesh" (Gal. 5:16). Furthermore: "For as many as are led by the Spirit of God, they are the sons of God" (Rom. 8:14).

When you compare the sorrow and defeat of our letter writer to Paul's counsel, it's like comparing light to darkness. God does not leave us without hope, without power, to overcome the devil. After He calls us to become saints, He does not leave us to wallow in the same sewer where He found us. "None need feel that they are powerless; for Christ declares, 'All power is given unto me in heaven and in earth.' He has promised that He will give this power to His workers. His power is to become their power. They are to link their souls with God."[3]

It is imperative that we change our mind-set from one of "victim" to "overcomer." Now is the time to focus our eyes upon the only One in whom victory is found. He can lead you out of the sewer. If lust for an inappropriate person is your giant, make Christ your passion!

Our letter writer also made a very revealing confession: "I have tried to stop but am unable." Look, let's face it—no one can stop, whatever the sins that plague our steps. But what we can do is choose to continually place ourselves in the pathway of Jesus Christ. We can choose to spend time with Him, basking in His cleansing fire. We can choose to reorder every priority of our lives and be His friend. This is the correct use of the human will. Our will is not a ballistic missile designed to take out giants. Our will is the gatekeeper of the mind, and the gatekeeper's job is to monitor traffic and to choose who and what goes in and out of our minds.

If we ever hope to win this battle with the giants and occupy the Promised Land, we must invite Jesus into our minds 24 hours a day, seven days a week. He has the missile defense system that has been proven fully capable of defending the human mind from every attack of Satan.

This is the promise: "I can do all things through Christ who strengthens me" (Phil. 4:13). Had Israel believed these words, they would not have died in the desert, leaving it to their children to destroy Jericho some 40 years later! "When you yield up your will to Christ, your life is hid with Christ in God. It is allied to the power which is above all principalities and powers. You have a strength from God that holds you fast to His strength; and a new life, even the life of faith, is possible to you."[4]

God told them that He had already given them the victory, but they lacked faith. They foolishly contradicted God: "Nevertheless the people who dwell in the land are strong; the cities are fortified and very large; moreover we saw the descendants of Anak there. . . . And we were like grasshoppers in our own sight" (Num. 13:28-33). In their sight, yes, but not God's. And it's always God's sight that matters.

Can you imagine God saying to you, "I will give you victory over every temptation, and I will transform you into My image," and your answer is "Pardon me, God, but have You considered this giant sin in my life?" Doesn't it sound a little ridiculous? We must take God at His word if we're going to make it to heaven.

Yes, it takes continuous effort on our part, because the "work of transformation from unholiness to holiness is a continuous one. Day by day God labors for man's sanctification, and man is to cooperate with Him, putting forth persevering efforts in the cultivation of right habits. He is to add grace to grace; and as he thus works on the plan of addition, God works for him on the plan of multiplication."[5]

Despite what the devil might tell us, you and I have only two choices in life, and victory can be obtained only by choosing one of them:

(1) **Die to Self → Old Man Destroyed → Does Not Serve Sin → Lives Forever**

(2) **Does Not Die Now → Old Man Lives → Continues to Sin → Dies Forever**

The apostle Paul said it best: "Do you not know that to whom you present yourselves slaves to obey, you are that one's slaves whom you obey, whether of *sin leading to death*, or of *obedience leading to righteousness*?" (Rom. 6:16). Do not ask God to guide your footsteps if you are not willing to move your feet, because you can't stay where you are and go with God.

A man in Jericho had been hearing a lot about Jesus, about His power to forgive sin and His power to transform hearts. God knew his desire and had sent His Spirit to work on the heart of Zacchaeus, the tax collector. On that day he was ready to do something about what he had heard. It was time to see Jesus with his own eyes.

Word traveled rapidly across the city to the taxman: the Healer was in Jericho. Zacchaeus shut the doors of his lucrative business and began his search for Christ. He had been dreaming about this moment for a long time.

It wasn't hard for Zacchaeus to find Jesus—just follow the massive throng of people jostling to get closer to Him. Unfortunately, Zacchaeus was such a short man that he couldn't see anything. What could he do? Well, for one thing, he'd come too far to be denied. He ran as far ahead and as fast as his short little legs could carry him.

Then he found it. Growing right in the middle of the street—a massive tree. As the crowd approached, he grabbed a branch and hoisted himself up onto a limb. He was thrilled! He'd now be head and shoulders above everyone else as the crowds began to converge beneath him. From his vantage point the people looked like an endless river of faces flowing around him.

Suddenly a voice from seemingly nowhere caught him off guard. It was not a tone that he'd normally heard as a taxman. It was caring, full of urgency: "Zacchaeus, make haste and come down, for today I must stay at your house" (Luke 19:5). Well, this was more than the little man could ever have imagined. It was such a powerful moment, it was recorded in the Bible.

Why did it happen? Lunch with the Master happened for Zacchaeus because he made a mindful decision earlier that day to place himself in the pathway of God. And God responded! That's what you and I must do every day, every hour. Only through the correct use of our will, accompanied by action, can we place ourselves where we can experience God.

The blessings of transformation come to those who not only make the choice to see God, but also act upon that choice and place themselves where God has the best opportunity to interact with them—in Bible study, prayer, and fellowship. "The measure of the Holy Spirit we receive will be proportioned to the measure of our desire and the faith exercised for it."[6]

In a most profound way that sycamore tree in Jericho was Zacchaeus' own tree of life. It was in the perfect location, and its limbs were at just the right height for him to climb up and see Jesus. It couldn't have been more perfect, and that's my point. The perfect tree enabled little Zacchaeus to find a way to secure an audience with Jesus at exactly the perfect time.

In my heart I believe God planned it that way, long before that day and long before Jericho became a city. God knew Zacchaeus would be hungering for His presence, so He found a way to help the little man. No, I can't be sure God planted the tree or sent an angel to defend it for 2,000 years, but I do know that God will find whatever way possible to meet with you. It's never an accident when it comes to God.

Indeed, it's no accident that you are reading this book. God is at the foot of your tree of life asking you to come down so He can stay in your home this very day. He is ready and able *if* you are willing to meet Him. "The will is the governing power in the nature of man, bringing all the other faculties under its sway. The will is not the taste or the inclination, but it is the deciding power, which works in the children of men unto obedience to God, or unto disobedience. . . . The will is . . . the power of . . . choice."[7]

That's why the devil is, right now, doing all he can to dissuade you from seeking intimacy with the Lord to experience transformation. He'll use every person around you, even people in the church, to distract and silence you. But don't give up; God is nearer to you than you think. He's ready to go the distance with you.

Another man in the vicinity of Jericho that day was destined to have an encounter with God as well. The locals knew him as Bartimaeus. Not only was he blind, he was poor, relegated to begging in the dust of the roadway.

Indeed, his day had begun as any other—in pain and in darkness. But a flicker of hope had started to smolder within him. Over time, he had been gathering bits and pieces of information concerning the one they called the Messiah. What he heard was exciting.

The reports circulating around Israel told of a Healer who broke up funerals by raising the dead. Bartimaeus heard that Jesus had walked through towns and that by the time He went out of the opposite gate, there wasn't a sick person left. Neither disease nor demons could resist His command to depart.

That day was not going to be like any other for Bartimaeus. The noise of the crowd was intense, even from his distant location. He began to ask others what the commotion was about, "and when he heard that it was Jesus of Nazareth, he began to cry out and say, 'Jesus, Son of David, have mercy on me!'" (Mark 10:47).

The Greek word translated "cry out" indicates he wasn't sobbing softly, but rather issuing a primal scream from the depths of his being. This was his one chance at transformation, and he was not going to miss the opportunity. For many, as he screamed at the top of his lungs, Bartimaeus was just noise pollution. Spiritually, they were as blind as the beggar was physically blind. The Messiah had been the focus of their hopes since they were born as a nation, but they didn't recognize Him or care to truly *see* Him when it mattered most.

The people warned the beggar to be quiet; they threatened him. But still he screamed again, "Son of David, have mercy on me!" (verse 48). And for his impassioned effort, he got an answer! "Jesus stood still and commanded him to be called. Then they called the blind man, saying to him, 'Be of good cheer. Rise, He is calling you.' And throwing aside his garment, he rose and came to Jesus" (verses 49, 50). Casting off his filthy rag covering, the blind man didn't allow anything to hinder him from the Savior.

Then Jesus "said to him, 'What do you want Me to do for you?' The blind man said to Him, '[Teacher], that I may receive my sight.' Then Jesus said to him, 'Go your way; your faith has made you well.' And immediately he received his sight and followed Jesus" (verses 51, 52).

The effect of coming into the presence of God is instantaneous; "instantly" the blind man "saw again." If we come near to Him, the radiance of His glory will shine into our lives and will begin to transform us instantaneously.

"His persevering faith is rewarded. Not only is physical sight restored, but the eyes of his understanding are opened. In Christ he sees his Redeemer, and the Sun of Righteousness shines into his soul. All who feel their need of Christ as did blind Bartimaeus, and who will be as earnest and determined as he was, will, like him, receive the blessing which they crave."[8]

Do you crave this blessing yet . . . or are you only almost convinced?

---

[1] See chapter 6.

[2] Italics supplied.

[3] Ellen G. White, *Colporteur Ministry* (Mountain View, Calif.: Pacific Press Pub. Assn., 1953), pp. 108, 109.

[4] E. G. White, *My Life Today*, p. 318.

[5] E. G. White, *The Acts of the Apostles*, p. 532.

[6] E. G. White, *God's Amazing Grace*, p. 207.

[7] E. G. White, *Child Guidance*, p. 209.

[8] E. G. White, *Sons and Daughters of God*, p. 126.

Chapter 19

Not Now—but Almost

From our viewpoint, their differences were as big as they get. Zacchaeus was rich and in need of nothing, while Bartimaeus was wretched and miserable, poor and blind. Interestingly, these polar opposites represent the people who populate God's final church just before Jesus returns—people whom He said must change!

Revelation 3:17-20 is riveting and heart-wrenching counsel from Jesus to His people near the end of time. Merging the characteristics of Zacchaeus and Bartimaeus, we say to God, "I am rich, have become wealthy, and have need of nothing," but in fact, we "do not know that [we] are wretched, miserable, poor, blind, and naked" (verse 17). It's hard-to-hear news, but it's full of hope too—because Zacchaeus and Bartimaeus were these things, but they put themselves in the proximity of Christ and were changed. This can be our experience if we call out to Jesus.

When we do call out, Jesus answers, "Buy from Me gold refined in the fire, that you may be rich; and white garments, that you may be clothed, that the shame of your nakedness may not be revealed; and anoint your eyes with eye salve, that you may see" (verse 18). It is all about God. He provides the transforming fire to burn away the sin in our lives. He clothes us with His garment of righteousness and anoints our eyes so we can see His army of light surrounding us to keep the giants at bay.

In response to His offer, we must "be zealous and repent" (verse 19). When we realize that we have been lied to by the devil regarding God's mighty ability to make us overcomers, we must cast ourselves at the foot of the cross and repent with the same gusto we once summoned in rebellion.

God is near. He says, "Behold, I stand at the door and knock. If anyone hears My voice and opens the door, I will come in to him and will dine with him" (verse 20). Perhaps you have already given entrance to the heavenly work crew and transformation is under way, but if not, Christ is knocking at your door, yearning for entrance not just to a single room, but to your whole house—your whole life.

If you desire Him as much as Zacchaeus and Bartimaeus did, you will have Him! The key is 100 percent surrender—not 25 percent, not 50 percent, and not a mere 99 percent. Transformation happens only when you give Him access to every corner of your life. "It is a perilous thing to allow an unchristian trait to live in the heart. One cherished sin will, little by little, debase the character, bringing all its nobler powers into subjection to the evil desire. The removal of one safeguard from the conscience, the indulgence of one evil habit, one neglect of the high claims of duty, breaks down the defenses of the soul and opens the way for Satan to come in and lead us astray."[1]

The Rusty Nail

As the story goes, a young couple was walking down the beach in Haiti with their young children. The two began to talk and dream of how nice it would be to own a house on the oceanfront. This desire grew in their hearts for some time until, one day, they decided to act.

They stopped at the home of an older fellow, living in the perfect house in the perfect place, and made him a cash offer on his home. "I don't want to sell," he said. They begged him to accept, but he refused.

Week after week they continued to plead with him—until one day he relented. They were absolutely thrilled, but he added one stipulation: "I maintain ownership of the nail above the front door." They hastily agreed to his demand and signed the papers that very week.

Soon the family moved in and enjoyed the house for many years. It was everything they had dreamed of. The beach was so much fun, so beautiful, and watching the children grow up in such a perfect environment was wonderful.

Then one day a knock came at the front door. It was the old man. "I want to buy the house back," he said. They utterly refused, confessing how much the whole family loved the house. Not another word was said as the old man walked away.

About a week later the family was in the kitchen eating when they began to smell something very foul. They looked everywhere, but couldn't find the source of the stench. To get away from it, they decided to leave the house and head to the beach. But as they were heading out the front door, they came face to face with a dead animal hanging in the doorway.

The father ran to get a stick and soon returned. Just as he reached up to unhook the carcass, someone shouted, "Stop!" The family peered into the distance and was stunned to see the old man standing afar off. "Did you forget? I own that nail. You can't touch that carcass; it is hanging on my nail." They knew he was right; they were legally bound to leave the carcass.

Eventually, the vile smell of rotting flesh became so intolerable that the family finally moved out of their home, selling it back to the old man. They couldn't believe they'd lost their dream home because of one solitary nail.

Likewise, many Christians are willing to gamble the dream of Paradise over one cherished sin. That's the sin you keep hidden under the bed, or in the closet, or in the locked room, or tucked away on your computer when the heavenly work crew comes to your home.

I once posted a question on Facebook to get my friends thinking. I wrote, "If life's journey is represented by a single roadway and the devil has the power to place temptations along that road in the form of enticing signs directing us toward a detour, what would your sign read? Example: Dillydally Alley."

I received a ton of great responses. I've chosen a few of them to share with you because they are good representations of the most tempting sins in our lives:

- Anxiety Avenue
- Self Center
- Lust Lane
- Impulsive Drive
- Pride Parkway
- Cheap Grace Way

- Depression Gulch
- Glutton Gorge
- Doubting Drive
- Pornography Parkway
- Lazy Lane
- Burnout Boulevard

I'm sure you could add a few more of your own.

This is why Jesus doesn't want to be just a passenger in your life, there to give you comfort only when you make the wrong turn down one of these roads. He wants to drive so that you avoid going the wrong way entirely. He alone has the ability to chauffeur you down the narrow way, driving you away from easy street. "Enter by the narrow gate," He said, "for wide is the gate and broad is the way that leads to destruction, and there are many who go in by it" (Matt. 7:13). And when God bids you to do anything, He enables you to do it. It's a promise.

Ruben

I met Ruben in Kenya. He grew up in a Christian home, but when he was old enough, he left home to become a long-haul truck driver. He was soon involved in all the things most drivers there were involved in and, over time, his faith and experience with the Lord were gone.

He explained, "My driving route took me through the heart of Tsavo National Park, the home of people-eating lions. Even though I live in a country of lions, I had never seen one. And I didn't want to, so I always made certain my schedule placed me in the park during daylight hours. I did not want to be there at night. But one day, the company had a scheduling problem and needed my help. They needed to get a load of sugarcane to the coast, which meant that my partner and I would have to travel through the park after dark—the best time for lions to hunt."

Ruben and his partner needed extra money, so they agreed to the job. They set out on their journey, and things were going fine until the truck began to sputter, lurch, and then—*nothing*. "I put the truck in gear, but there was no response. We had lost the driveshaft. No matter what I did, we weren't going anywhere." The truck was dead. But even worse, it was dead in the middle of Tsavo Park in the darkness of night.

Ruben called the company, but they said they wouldn't make it out to him until morning. So the two partners did the only thing they had left to do: roll up the windows and settle in for the night.

Ruben thought a little music would be nice, so he turned on the radio. "I accidentally tuned to a Christian radio program, but I shut it off right away because I really didn't want to listen to the preacher calling for listeners to come home, to come back to God." So Ruben and his partner talked to pass the time—that is, until a huge male lion pushed his whiskered face against the glass of Ruben's window. After its short inspection, the lion soon wandered toward the front of the truck and met up with a female lion and her cubs.

As Ruben relayed the next part of the story, I could see it still haunted him. "The male lion began moving slowly in our direction. He then put his massive paws up on the front of our truck and stared in at the two of us. We were frightened. He got down and seemed to be heading back up the road when, all of a sudden, he turned and charged the truck. With one powerful leap, he flew through the air and slammed into the windshield, shattering it into pieces."

The lion moved like lightning; razor-sharp claws and a giant paw snatched Ruben's partner from his seat and yanked him from the truck.

Amid the harrowing screams for help, the lion began eating the man from his legs upward as Ruben watched. His fear paralyzed him. All he could do was shout, "Lord, save me! I'll do anything You want—just save me!"

As Ruben's desperate prayer continued, the lion finished its meal, rose up, put his paws on the windowless dash, and looked directly into his face. Then, still crying out to God, Ruben saw car lights. The car stopped near the scene; perhaps the driver was too frightened to continue on. Yet undeterred, the lion backed up and prepared to charge again. But instead of charging at Ruben, the lion jumped on top of the truck cab, where it would stay for the entire night.

The next morning, help finally arrived to chase away the lions. A tiny woman then got out of the car that had stopped and poked her finger in the chest of the six-foot-three-inch Ruben and asked, "Are you a Christian?"

Ruben responded, "I guess so."

She said, "You need to go home, study, and pray!" She then turned and left.

He didn't know who the woman was. When I pressed him about who she was, he said calmly, "I think it was my angel." What happened after this stunning experience? Well, today Ruben is now a faithful seller of Christian books, spreading the gospel of a soon-coming Savior. Our camera crew was so moved by his story that we pitched in and bought him a motorcycle so he could cover more territory for God all across Kenya.

The apostle Peter experienced the ripping fangs of the devil and was well qualified to share these words: "Be sober, be vigilant; because your adversary the devil walks about like a roaring lion, seeking whom he may devour" (1 Peter 5:8). Make no mistake: The devil wants to destroy you. But you also have a foolproof protection plan. If you will submit to God and rely upon Him, you can "resist the devil and he will flee from you" (James 4:7). This is a product backed up by an eternal warranty, but you must buy the goods for the warranty to go into force.

"Everyone who thirsts, come to the waters; and you who have no money, come, buy and eat. . . . Seek the Lord while He may be found, call upon Him while He is near. Let the wicked forsake his way, and the unrighteous man his thoughts; let him return to the Lord, and He will have mercy on him; and to our God, for He will abundantly pardon" (Isa. 55:1-9).

I believe this story of the lions and the many others I have shared in this book reveal that God is at work around the world, calling and preparing people to joyfully stand and welcome Him at His soon coming.

I received a call from Sweden not long ago from a woman who identified herself as a Catholic. She said, "I watched your program for a year, and it scared me." Why? "Because I saw how God was working in the lives of those people you interviewed. He wasn't working in my life that way." It had so moved her, she was baptized!

I often get asked, "Why isn't God working like that here in America?" Well, as a matter of fact, He is.

An American Miracle Story

My wife and I were attending the Generation of Youth for Christ convention in Houston, where thousands of young people boarded buses bound for area neighborhoods. There were so many wanting to witness for the Lord that there weren't enough buses to transport them all. Not getting discouraged, one small group prayed about their situation and decided to walk around the nearby business district and see whom the Lord would lead them to. It didn't take long for God to respond to their faith.

While they were standing on a street corner, a city bus suddenly pulled up to the curb. The driver jumped out, leaving his passengers sitting in the bus at the unscheduled stop, and ran toward the team and excitedly asked, "Are you Christians?"

"Yes!" they responded in kind.

Then with urgency, the driver pleaded, "How can I be saved?"

Of course, you and I both know the answer to the bus driver's question. But after the Lord has done His work of salvation, what happens next? What questions do we need to be asking? Here are just a few for you to think about:

- Are we living out all that we know God requires of us in appreciation for His saving work in our lives?
- Have we surrendered fully to Him—without reserve?
- Are we going to stay a worm, or are we, by God's transforming power, going to become glorious butterflies?

It's Not Convenient Right Now . . .

Because of his faith, the apostle Paul found himself in the prison of Felix the Roman procurator. Felix was once a Greek slave of Nero until he bought his own freedom. A self-made man, he was corrupt and power hungry. He had even enticed his present wife, the Jew Drusilla, to leave King Azizus and marry him. "She was prevailed on," the historian Josephus records, "to transgress the laws of her forefathers, and to marry Felix."

Paul was eventually brought before the two sinners, and he addressed his audience with heavenly borne conviction. He spoke to them "concerning the faith in Christ. . . . [He] reasoned about righteousness, self-control, and the judgment to come" (Acts 24:24, 25).

Paul spoke about the character that all who wish to receive eternal life must possess; he spoke these words to a man who was perfectly corrupt. He spoke about temperance to a man and a woman who knew only lust, and he spoke about the coming judgment when even kings will be naked before the great throne of God. He spoke about a time when every sin done in secret will be a spectacle to unseen worlds.

The Bible record states that Felix *trembled* at this (verse 25, KJV). This mighty governor of Israel, who was never before inclined to discuss the God of the Jews, now saw the results of his life of sin—such that he shook uncontrollably at the thought of standing before God. But instead of responding to the call, to the promptings of the Holy Spirit, he composed his thoughts and said to Paul, "Go away for now; when I have a convenient time I will call for you" (verse 25).

How many times have we said to God, "This is not a convenient time; maybe later"? When the Holy Spirit speaks to us, it is a dangerous thing to not respond immediately!

Felix was later torn from power, narrowly escaping death. Yet he would eventually succumb to his evil. Some historians believe his third wife poisoned him. Drusilla faired no better; she and her son were at Pompeii when Mount Vesuvius spewed a gargantuan cloud of poisonous fire and ash across the city. Both died as the suffocating heat, smoke, and dust laid a blanket of death across the landscape.

For Felix and Drusilla, a more "convenient time" never came.

When Paul later appeared before King Agrippa, he asked a pointed question: "Do you believe the prophets? I know that you do believe" (Acts 26:27). Since the king was a Jew, Paul didn't wait for the answer but proceeded to the proof that Jesus of Nazareth was the Messiah the prophets spoke about.

Amid the outburst that followed Paul's bold sermon, a man named Festus called the apostle mad. But even still, Agrippa teetered on the edge of eternity, his heart touched like that of Judas' in the upper room. Deep inside he thrilled at the thought of inviting Jesus into his life—but he was a king, and Satan paraded every possible negative before the mind of this powerful man. Agrippa eventually answered, "You almost persuade me to become a Christian" (verse 28).

The famous TV secret agent Maxwell Smart would often say, "Missed it by that much!" But this was no sitcom. Unfortunately for Agrippa, it doesn't matter how close we come if we miss transformation and heaven. Almost is really nothing at all.

On another occasion, Paul was in the city of Philippi when he encountered a woman with a demon. She had been bringing her masters a lot of money because of her gift, but Paul cast the demon out of her. This angered her owners, and, in turn, stirred up a crowd against Paul. The authorities got involved and threw Paul in jail for his own protection!

Amazing. Paul had just performed a good deed and was now stuck in a dark, dank, rat-infested prison, anchored to the walls with cold iron shackles. But since Paul and his companion, Silas, had the Light of the world abiding within their hearts, they began to sing.

Suddenly the rafters began to shake, the walls began to quake, and the floors started to heave and sway as the angels joined in the sweet chorus. This praise chorus literally brought the house down . . .

"Suddenly there was a great earthquake, so that the foundations of the prison were shaken; and immediately all the doors were opened and everyone's chains were loosed. And the keeper of the prison, awaking from sleep and seeing the prison doors open, supposing the prisoners had fled, drew his sword and was about to kill himself. But Paul called with a loud voice, saying, 'Do yourself no harm, for we are all here'" (Acts 16:26-28).

The jailer grabbed a torch, ran into Paul's cellblock, and ushered the two Christians outside the demolished prison. As soon as they stopped, the jailer begged, "What must I do to be saved?" (verse 30). It was exactly the same response of that Houston bus driver!

So I ask you, where do you fit in among these stories? Here are three possible responses to God's call on your life:
1. This really isn't a convenient time to accept You, God; I'll get back to You.
2. You have almost convinced me to yield my life to You; I'm "that" close.
3. Lord, what must I do to be saved?

Option three is the fully humble, die-to-self, 100 percent surrender to God. Anything less is a losing proposition. Remember, all you need to do is the choosing, and our loving Lord will provide *everything* else. "God wishes us to have the mastery over ourselves. But He cannot help us *without our consent and cooperation.* The divine Spirit works through the powers and faculties given to man. Of ourselves, we are not able to bring the purposes and desires and inclinations into harmony with the will of God; but '*if we are willing to be made willing,*' the Savior will accomplish this for us."[2]

I have prayed many times in my life, "Lord, make me willing to be made willing." God has answered that prayer for me, and He will answer it for you if you ask. And soon, all of His transformation power will reside in you. Then you will have the assurance that "when He is revealed, we shall be like Him" (1 John 3:2). Armed with that assurance, one day you will look up into a blazing sky and say, "Behold, this is our God; we have waited for Him, and He will save us" (Isa. 25:9).

Always keep in mind: It's all about God! There are no invincible giants when you are standing on the shoulders of the Almighty. God and you are an unbeatable team! May your blessings be multiplied as you shed the old and become the new—transformed into the King's perfect image.

> "*Now to Him who is able to keep you from stumbling, and to present you faultless before the presence of His glory with exceeding joy, to God our Savior, who alone is wise, be glory and majesty, dominion and power, both now and forever. Amen*" (Jude 24, 25).

---

[1] Ellen G. White, *Patriarchs and Prophets* (Mountain View, Calif.: Pacific Press Pub. Assn., 1890), p. 452.

[2] E. G. White, *The Acts of the Apostles*, p. 482. (Italics supplied.)